CJNG

A QUICK GUIDE TO MEXICO'S DEADLIEST CARTEL

BY

CHRIS DALBY

WORLD OF CRIME

For more about World of Crime, please visit www.worldofcrime.net

Editing by Caroline Booker

Designed by Immaculate Studios

eBook ISBN: 9789083423906

Paperback ISBN: 9789083423913

Audiobook ISBN: 9789083423913

Welcome to World of Crime's Guide to the Jalisco Cartel New Generation (CJNG)

So what is this guide for?

These guides provide short but comprehensive insights into the most influential organised crime networks currently in existence.

Each chapter is dedicated to a separate aspect of these groups' activities, their criminal economies and the threats they pose.

The World of Crime chose to dedicate this first guide to the Jalisco Cartel New Generation, better known as the CJNG.

We spend time in the avocado fields of Michoacán to understand how the wealthy Valencia family grew to become one of the most influential criminal clans in Mexico, which in turn would later give birth to the CJNG.

We consider the cult of personality around one of the most wanted men in the world, Nemesio Oseguera Cervantes, alias "El Mencho," the highly elusive CJNG kingpin.

Chapter by chapter, the World of Crime breaks down each of the CJNG's economic pillars, including fentanyl, meth, cocaine and smaller forms of income. We then take a tour of Mexico, revealing the CJNG's status and actions in each Mexican state, as well as in the United States, and around the world.

Welcome to World of Crime.

WORLD OF CRIME

World of Crime publishes regular Guides to Organized Crime, breaking down the inner workings of the most influential criminal networks in existence. To stay up-to-date about all our coming releases, please subscribe to our newsletter at:

https://seasonsofcrime.com

Our newsletter also hosts the Seasons of Crime where we explore little-known ways in which organized crime influences important sectors of politics, technology, business and society.

Upcoming Seasons include *Organized Crime and AI*, *Organized Crime and Climate Change*, and *Organized Crime and Children*.

To reach out to us directly for collaborations, rights, or other business inquiries, please write to info@worldofcrime.net.

Table of Contents

INTRODUCTION

Why is Mexico's Jalisco Cartel New Generation (Cártel de Jalisco Nueva Generación - CJNG) worthy of being the first criminal group featured in the World of Crime's Guides to Organized Crime?

Because there's no other cartel quite like it.

Why?

First, there's the real-world impact. The CJNG is one of two truly transnational cartels in Mexico, able to project its strength in almost every part of the country. Since 2012, when it began rapidly expanding across the country, the CJNG has been focused on one goal: to become Mexico's dominant criminal actor.

The group makes almost formal declarations of war when it expands into a new state, warning criminal rivals and corrupt authorities of brutal consequences to come.

Then come the drugs. The CJNG is responsible for a large proportion of all fentanyl, methamphetamine, cocaine and heroin plaguing the United States, Mexico and far beyond.

In the US, the CJNG has a well-oiled network of intermediaries and connections to local drug traffickers, which enable its products to be spread nationwide.

In Ecuador, it has contributed to that country's descent into chaos, funding its gang war with money and weapons in exchange for a glut of cocaine.

A web of international commerce allows CJNG to source vast quantities of chemical precursors from China and India, sell large quantities of meth to Europe and Oceania, and launder its illicit proceeds in a variety of ways.

Then come the headlines. More than any other Mexican criminal group, the CJNG seems to crave the limelight. It has an undeniable talent for PR. From blowing army helicopters in the sky to military-style parades of their arsenals, the CJNG likes to be noticed.

Even their leader is a source of constant speculation. Nemesio Oseguera Cervantes, alias "Mencho," is one of the world's most wanted men. At least outwardly, his men seem to have a fanatical devotion to him, as he is named in almost every video or message issued by the CJNG. But there are almost no photos of him. Authorities and criminal rivals are unsure if he's even still alive.

Then come all the other ways to make money. Organized crime is the most adaptable line of business in the world. But even with that in mind, the CJNG is a real journeyman cartel.

Its members grow marijuana, produce meth and fentanyl, extort money from avocado and lime growers, shake down hotel owners, steal gasoline, bomb enemies in the skies using drones, smuggle migrants across Mexico's north and south borders, buy tons of cocaine a year, and pay for it in cash and weapons.

This very diversity has helped it survive. In a country where large criminal networks see a well-established cycle of growth and fragmentation, the CJNG has survived for over a decade.

It is the living embodiment of criminal opportunism.

THE CJNG'S ORIGINS

Important Names to Remember:

Armando Valencia Cornelio, alias "Maradona," founder of the Milenio Cartel and leader until his arrest in 2003.

Nemesio Oseguera Cervantes, alias "Mencho," founder and current leader of the CJNG, one of Mexico's most powerful kingpins.

Ignacio Coronel Villarreal, former Sinaloa Cartel boss in the city of Guadalajara, killed by Mexican security forces in 2010.

Osiel Cardenas Guillén, leader of the Gulf Cartel, former ally then enemy of the Milenio Cartel.

Carlos Rosales Mendoas, alias "Tísico," a powerful drug trafficker and founder of La Familia Michoacana.

***This chapter covers the history of the CJNG until 2015, the year when it became fully recognized as a criminal organization with a national and international reach. The rest of the CJNG's journey is told throughout the rest of the book, divided by topic.**

If you throw a stone at a random farm or house in the mountains around the town of Aguililla, there's a good chance you'll hit property belonging to someone with the family name Valencia.

There are thousands of Valencias in the mountains of Mexico's southwestern state of Michoacán.

This part of Mexico has been at the center of virtually every major period in the country's history. Conquistadors burned chieftains alive here, insurgents gathered here to fight the Spanish, and miners came to delve for gold, silver, copper and iron.

Besides its historical importance, Michoacán is an ideal location for drug production and trafficking. Its fertile mountains are great hiding spots for growing marijuana and opium poppy. The state has a lengthy Pacific coastline and holds one of Mexico's largest seaports. It is just a few hours' drive from Mexico City and is well-connected to highways heading to the US border.

Certain maize and bean farmers, the Valencias among them, spotted the potential of the drug business early. Exactly how early is difficult to ascertain. Marijuana and opium poppy production was a popular means of subsistence for farming communities in the northern state of Sinaloa in the 1940s and its influence gradually spread south.

By the late 1950s, marijuana and opium poppy plantations had started appearing around farmsteads in the town of Dos Aguas, a small village west of the town of Aguililla. These plantations grew steadily until the 1970s, when a man known as José Valencia was already a reliable supplier of marijuana and opium poppy for larger groups in northern Mexico, especially around Sinaloa.[1]

The decision to marry avocados with drugs would set the stage for complex cartel dynamics, which continue to kill thousands fifty years later. It would contribute to making Aguililla a focal point for cartel violence, cement Michoacán as one of the most violent states in Mexico, and give rise to the most murderous of Mexican cartels: the CJNG.

Avocadonomics

The avocado boom of the 1980s would give enterprising members of the family the connections they needed to expand.[2] Luis Valencia had extensive avocado plantations around the town of Aguililla, while his cousin, Armando Valencia Cornelio, had the same plantations in the municipality of Uruapan, about 100 kilometres to the northeast.

They owned at least six avocado farms and several packing plants for the fruit. The two towns offered very convenient hubs for the Valencias' operations. They were remote enough not to be constantly bothered by authorities, and were close to Mexico City, ports along the Pacific coast and major highways north.

A series of socio-economic and political changes set in motion during the 1980s and 1990s allowed the Valencias to rapidly expand their licit and illicit businesses hand-in-hand.

First, Michoacán's agricultural economics were severely damaged by a rapid shift in Mexico's trade policies.

The spread of international free trade and a trend toward government deregulation had a cascading effect on how Mexican farmers could both sell their products and get access to financing.[3] State support melted away and banks set far harsher rates for financing.

Unable to adapt, many farmers were forced to sell their land or find other ways to finance themselves. The Valencias were all too happy to step into their breach.

By this point, the Valencia family was providing for hundreds of people, in their avocado farms, packing plants and marijuana plantations. Young children would leave school early to go to work for the family. Mencho reportedly dropped out of school and went to work as an avocado picker on the Valencias' properties at the age of eleven.

With their communities struggling, the family expanded. If a farmer needed to sell their land, the Valencias needed more room for avocado trees and marijuana plants. The family made other investments in the community, including providing financial loans to those who couldn't get bank loans, and their power and respect grew accordingly.

Secondly, the US fell in love with avocados.

In the 1980s, the Valencia family had nationwide connections to sell their fruit, and smuggle drugs within the cargos, across Mexico. But they could not sell their avocados north of the border.

This was partly because of a pesky creature, the avocado seed weevil. This long-nosed pest was rampant among Michoacán's avocado crops for decades. Fearing that the weevil could contaminate its own crops, the US banned all imports of Mexican avocados in 1914. This ban lasted almost 80 years.

In 1992, the signing of the North American Free Trade Agreement (NAFTA) inadvertently played right into the Valencia family's hands. In December of that year, US President George W. Bush, Mexico's President Carlos Salinas de Gortari, and Canadian Prime Minister Brian Mulroney signed the final agreement. This allowed most Mexican exports to enter their northern neighbours without any tariffs.

Negotiations for agricultural produce had been particularly difficult. Agricultural interest groups such as the Florida Farm Bureau and the Canadian Wheat Board had major concerns about how letting in Mexican produce would affect their home markets. These concerns were progressively smoothed over in separate and torturous agreements.[4]

One way to ensure quality control for Mexican produce was to ensure that certain areas with a heavy concentration of one crop would be closely inspected. At the head of that list were avocados in Michoacán.

This made sense. Mexico accounted for over 30% of the global crop at the time. And Michoacán provided an overwhelming majority, or just under 75% of Mexico's avocado crop. Avocado producers in Michoacán, likely including the Valencias, were helped by a US-backed program to eradicate the avocado seed weevil.

The Valencias saw an explosion in their export options.

The Milenio Cartel is Born

In the 1980s, Armando Valencia Cornelio, now known by his alias "Maradona," spotted a gap in his knowledge. He knew the avocado business well enough, but his knowledge of drug trafficking was limited.

He became a criminal journeyman. In 1985, he was reportedly living in Redwood, California, a sister city to Aguililla with a heavy diaspora from that part of Michoacán.[5]

While there is little information about what Armando did in California or how many years he spent there, one can speculate that it was related to the drug trade. Several figures from the Milenio Cartel, including Mencho, were in California in the mid-1980s and known to be involved in selling Mexican heroin and marijuana as well as producing and selling meth.

Armando Valencia Cornelio, alias "Maradona"

Armando also worked for a time in the mid-1980s for Miguel Ángel Félix Gallardo, founder of the Guadalajara Cartel and one of Mexico's most successful drug traffickers. After Gallardo was arrested in 1989, and his

Guadalajara Cartel broke apart, Armando found his way to the Juarez Cartel and the Carrillo Fuentes family.

Besides a single arrest warrant against him in Michoacán in 1990 for possession of cocaine, there is little record of Armando's role within the Guadalajara and Juarez Cartels. But he was certainly in the right place and the right time.

Gallardo and the Carrillo Fuentes brothers were highly successful drug traffickers, with the former helping to pioneer the Colombia-Mexico-US pipeline with Pablo Escobar, and the latter cornering a large part of that same drug market after Escobar was killed in 1993.

But eventually Armando, along with his cousin, Luis, saw room for his own outfit. Instead of simply supplying other cartels with marijuana and opium poppy, they created their own.

At first, the new group seemed more focused on collaboration than competition. The Valencia cousins began to progressively take over territory for marijuana plantations along Mexico's Pacific coast in the states of Jalisco, Colima and Nayarit. The money made from their expanded drug operations was laundered through the avocado trade. The group even became known as Los Reyes del Aguacate (The Avocado Kings), again blurring the lines between legitimate and illicit business.[6]

They also cultivated close ties to two larger groups along the border, the Juárez Cartel and the Gulf Cartel, to help set up their first drug connections to the United States. Mexican authorities at the time seemed uncertain how to view the Avocado Kings. The group was first created in the late 1990s, but some police reports show the Valencias as a cell of the Juárez Cartel, rather than being independent.[7] This is likely because Armando maintained close ties to his former bosses along the US border.

It was also tricky for authorities to take major steps against the Valencias. First, Mexico had significantly larger drug trafficking threats to focus on at the time. The Guadalajara Cartel had splintered off into several smaller but powerful constituent groups, including the Tijuana, Juárez and Sinaloa Cartels.

Second, the Valencia family had deep roots in the mountains of central and northern Michoacán, with corrupt connections to police, politicians, prosecutors, and more.

Third, investigating the group wasn't easy. There were thousands of people named Valencia in the mountains of Michoacán, making it rather difficult to investigate which were part of any illegal group.

Enter Escobar

The Milenio Cartel quietly became a mainstay along Mexico's Pacific coast and established a profitable drug production pipeline for marijuana and heroin in Michoacán as well as the nearby states of Jalisco, Colima and Nayarit. This also gave the family prime access to the port of Lázaro Cárdenas, one of Mexico's largest ports and a trade hub on the country's Pacific Coast.

This caught the attention of a powerful potential partner: Pablo Escobar and his Medellín Cartel in Colombia.

Following the fall of Gallardo and the break-up of the Guadalajara Cartel, Escobar needed new Mexican partners to move cocaine shipments to the United States. Other pretenders could move huge quantities of cocaine but were being weakened by internal feuds.

One of Escobar's US-based lieutenants, Fabio Ochoa, brokered the relationship with the Valencias. Even after Escobar died in a hail of bullets in 1993, Ochoa continued to use the Milenio Cartel. Charging documents against Ochoa, following his arrest and extradition to the US in 2001, state that around 30 tons of cocaine were being handled by the Valencia network every month between 1997 and 1999.

According to one investigation, the Valencias used their presence along the Pacific Coast to place cocaine loads onto boats, often tuna fishing vessels, heading north to the United States.[9] DEA documents tell of shipments of Colombian cocaine being sent by Armando to New York City every single week.[10]

Another arrest provided a glimpse into the power the Valencias had amassed. In August 2001, Gino Brunetti, a Colombian trafficker, accused of supervising much of the flow of Colombian cocaine going through Mexico and the US, was arrested in Cancun. He promptly started collaborating with Mexican and American authorities, providing information in exchange for a reduced sentence.

A snippet from his interview with Mexican police is revealing:

- "Do you know which cartel is moving the most drugs right now?" Brunetti asked the prosecutors.

- "No… to which cartel are you referring?"

- "The Valencias, the Milenio Cartel," said the Colombian.

- "Who are the Valencias?"

- "They are the most important and powerful importers of drugs to the United States."

This cocaine trade success greatly accelerated the Milenio Cartel's ability to move up the criminal ladder. In the late 1990s into the early 2000s, Armando's Milenio Cartel may have moved up to one-third of all the cocaine consumed in the United States.

The future of the cartel seemed bright.

The Love Triangle Which Changed Everything

This level of control allowed the Milenio Cartel to strike up relations with the next generation of upcoming drug traffickers in Mexico.

Now, the next part of the Milenio Cartel's history gets quite complex. Let's first introduce a couple of new faces.

Osiel Cárdenas Guillén had quickly become one of the most important drug traffickers in Mexico and controlled significant access points to the United States. His criminal outfit, known as the Gulf Cartel, was one of Mexico's oldest drug trafficking groups and mostly controlled the northeastern state of Tamaulipas and border crossings into Texas.

Carlos Rosales Mendoza was an influential Michoacán drug trafficker who worked as a go-between the Valencias and Osiel. Rosales had been involved in Michoacán's crime scene for decades and was a particularly close friend to the Gulf Clan leader.

Osiel Cárdenas Guillén

In the early 2000s, Nuevo Laredo was host to a web of drug trafficking dynamics and brutal feuds involving prominent cartels, which is far too complex to unravel here. We will focus on the parts that directly involve the Milenio Cartel.

The Gulf Cartel and Milenio Cartel had become tentative neighbours in the early 2000s. As part of their Escobar-fuelled expansion, the Valencias had established a presence in the Mexican border city of Nuevo Laredo in Tamaulipas.

Carlos Rosales Mendoza had been crucial to the early partnership. He had introduced Osiel to the Valencia clan and the two groups collaborated on sending a steady flow of marijuana and cocaine north to Tamaulipas.

Rosales' ability to work with the Milenio Cartel was facilitated by love. He became close with Armando's chief of security, none other than the future leader of the CJNG, Nemesio Oseguera Cervantes, alias "Mencho."

Mencho had a cousin, Inés Oseguera. According to Rosales, they met at a cockfight in Michoacán. Rosales had travelled there to arrange a deal for the Valencias to sell 50 tons of cocaine to the Gulf Cartel. Shortly after, they got married and had a son, Rosales told Mexican journalist J. Jesús Lemus in a genuinely moving interview from prison years later.[11]

"There is nothing in this world that makes a man happier than having a son with the woman he loves. Inés made me the happiest man in the world," he said.

But their love did not last long. Inés attracted the attention of a powerful rival: none other than Armando Valencia Cornelio, the head of the Milenio Cartel.

"I never thought the friendship between Osiel, Armando Valencia and myself would finish in disgrace. The love of a woman ended up separating us," said Rosales.

While Rosales described Cárdenas Guillén as having always been respectful to his wife, Armando was not. "As soon as he met her, his eyes were shining. For her, given what happened later, I imagined things moved as well," said Rosales.

Rosales described the boundless hatred he developed for all Valencias, calling himself a "demon wounded by love."

He began a hunt on all Valencias and anyone connected to them, promising to pay a $20,000 bounty to anyone who would kill a Valencia. He even told his men to kill their dogs.

Rosales had a powerful ally ready to help. While loyal to his friend, Cárdenas Guillén had his own reasons for turning on the Valencias. Removing them and having Rosales dominate the Michoacán drug scene would allow Cárdenas Guillén to partially control one of Mexico's principal sources of marijuana and opium poppy.

First, he moved to break any Milenio influence in Nuevo Laredo. At the time, the Valencias depended on an alliance with a drug trafficker named Dionisio García, alias "El Chacho." Anyone seeking to move drugs through the city had to pay him off, and he had developed a close relationship with the Valencias.

A cocaine deal involving Armando Cornelio Valencia, Cárdenas Guillén and García allegedly went wrong in early 2002. There are several versions of this story. Some media reports state that the Milenio Cartel trusted García to deliver the cocaine to Cárdenas Guillén, but that he kept it for himself. Others say the Gulf Cartel simply stole it.

Either way, Cárdenas Guillén wanted García dead. In February 2022, he unleashed his most powerful weapon: the Zetas. The name of the Zetas has become legendary as one of Mexico's most brutal criminal groups. But they began as a ruthlessly efficient hit squad made up of highly trained former members of Mexican special forces. Moving into Nuevo Laredo, 50 to 60 Zetas allegedly routed 300 men working for García.

García fled Nuevo Laredo for Monterrey, a large city to the south, but by May 2002, he had been found, kidnapped, tortured and killed.

Cárdenas Guillén didn't stop there. To help clear out the Valencias, around 300 Zetas invaded Michoacán to work alongside Rosales' group, known as La Familia Michoacana.

This began a horrific cycle of violence from which Michoacán has never escaped. In just a few months in 2002, around 250 people were killed, including several political officials known to be close to the Valencia family, according to Lemus.[12]

But while the violence endured, the three men at the centre of the war all soon faded. Armando survived an assassination attempt by Rosales but was arrested in a military operation in 2003. He was jailed in Mexico until 2012 before being extradited to the US, where he was sentenced to over 19 years in prison for drug trafficking. He was released early in 2020 from a maximum-security facility in Kentucky, allegedly because he was suffering from lymphoma.

Osiel was arrested in 2003 after a shootout with Mexican soldiers, extradited to the United States in 2007, and sentenced to 25 years in prison for a number of charges, including trafficking large quantities of marijuana and cocaine. He is scheduled to be released in 2024.

Carlos Rosales' loyalty to Cárdenas Guillén did not end once the Gulf Cartel leader was behind bars. He was arrested in 2004 while allegedly planning a daring mission to break his friend out of. He was jailed for ten years in Mexico, released in 2014, but was found tortured and killed in Michoacán in 2015, likely by a rival criminal group.

The Milenio Survivors Head North

After the arrest of Maradona, his nephews, Oscar Orlando and Juan Nava Valencia, took control of the Milenio Cartel. Known respectively as El Lobo (The Wolf) and El Tigre (The Tiger), Oscar Orlando and Juan steered the Milenio Cartel through a difficult period.

The two new leaders faced a bitter reality check. The war with the Zetas was going poorly. For the first time in years, the Milenio Cartel was no longer the premier criminal power in Michoacán. From 2003 to 2005, hundreds of murders in Michoacán were connected to the Zetas-Milenio feud. Although Rosales had been arrested, his Familia Michoacana were beginning to dominate the state's drug scene and were producing large quantities of methamphetamine.

Many of those dying were Valencias, and they were being hunted across the country. In January 2005, Felipe Erick Espinosa Valencia, a Milenio lieutenant, and two of his cousins were among five people gunned down at a ranch in the faraway southern state of Chiapas.

Then, in August 2005, a strike closer to home. About 250 people were gathered for a cockfighting event at a horse-racing track in Tonalá, Jalisco. Assailants threw two fragmentation grenades into the crowd, killing five people and injuring 30 more. The property was owned by the Valencias and numerous family members were in attendance. Mencho's cousin, Saúl, was among the dead.[13]

This also marked the first time such grenades were used in a cartel attack in Mexico. The military-style arsenal also rapidly led the police to blame the attack on the Zetas.

The pressure was getting too much. The Valencias needed help. To the north, the Milenio Cartel had some presence in the states of Jalisco and Nayarit, from where they supplied a number of larger groups, including the Sinaloa Cartel, with marijuana and heroin.

It was time for the unthinkable to happen. The Valencias would have to leave Michoacán.

But the retreat would not be directionless. The Milenio Cartel maintained strong relations with one of their drug trafficking partners to the north: the Sinaloa Cartel, then led by Joaquín Guzmán Loera, alias "El Chapo."

The two sides came to a deal. The Valencias would become a type of criminal vassal to the larger cartel. Both sides stood to benefit. The Milenio Cartel obtained protection and shelter, while the Sinaloa Cartel would gain the Valencias' extensive experience in synthetic drug production and financial savvy.

El Chapo knew just the man to keep the new arrivals in line. They were placed under the leadership of his father-in-law, Ignacio Coronel, alias "Nacho," the Sinaloa Cartel's chief in Jalisco's capital, Guadalajara.

Coronel shared a common love with the Valencias - the production of methamphetamine - and was known as El Rey del Cristal (The King of Crystal).

However, Michoacán was not a major priority for the Sinaloa Cartel. While the Valencias kept a foothold in the west of the state, the Sinaloa Cartel did not commit significant forces to help them reclaim their land. Instead, the Milenio Cartel's focus would shift to helping their new patrons bring shipments of chemical precursors needed to make methamphetamine from China, laundering its funds, and helping extend its control to other parts of the country.

Any Milenio stragglers found in Michoacán were still at risk though. In April 2007, Ventura Valencia, Armando's cousin and a highly influential voice in the family, phoned his wife to tell her he was on his way to Aguililla. He never made it. His body was found three days later, bearing signs of torture and with a message nailed to his chest. The message threatened various Milenio Cartel leaders, including Mencho.

This appears to have been the first time Mencho was publicly identified as a prominent leader within the group, with the Mexican press identifying him as the chief gunman for the Valencias.[14]

The Milenio-Sinaloa alliance held for a few years, with the Valencia family supporting the Sinaloa Cartel in a brutal war with the Beltrán-Leyva Organization (BLO).

But the Valencias would soon see more changes at the top. Their top commanders would fall one after another.

Within a few short months between 2009 and 2010, El Lobo and El Tigre were both arrested.[15] This only precipitated the internal collapse of the Milenio Cartel.

The two brothers had been crucial to maintaining unity in the group during tough times, including the retreat from Michoacán, their subservience to the Sinaloa Cartel, and accepting the orders of Coronel.

With the cartel still reeling from the two arrests, they then lost their patron. On July 29, 2010, Coronel himself was killed in a brutal shootout with navy troops in Zapopan, Jalisco.

These arrests and deaths have been the object of much debate. Media reports have suggested that Coronel and Mencho worked together to remove the brothers following a dispute. Allegations that Mencho periodically betrayed rivals to authorities have dogged him for decades.

In one account, journalist Lemus suggests that Coronel and the Nava Valencia brothers had plotted to take over cocaine trafficking routes in Quintana Roo to have better access to cocaine coming from Colombia. This supposedly angered the Juárez Cartel who worked with Genaro García Luna, then Mexico's Minister of Public Security, to have Coronel removed.[16]

The truth of these accounts may never be settled. But without their unifying presence, the Milenio Cartel began to fragment.

Mencho's Contested Ascent

Mencho saw a chance to become the boss. He certainly had the credentials to become so. Affiliated with the Valencias since early childhood, he had served the clan dutifully. He had acted as head of security for Maradona, and then as a leading hitman under the orders of Ignacio Coronel and the Sinaloa Cartel.

He had also married Valencia royalty. His wife, Rosalinda Gonzalez Valencia, was the eldest sister of the Cuinis, a huge brood of siblings who were becoming highly influential in the Valencia family. Mencho's brother-in-law and closest ally, Abigael, was a financial whiz and money laundering expert. Mencho also had the support of Erick Valencia Salazar, alias "El 85," another leading light within the family.[17]

But there was dissent in the ranks. Suspicions had begun circulating that Mencho had secured his rise up the ranks by conveniently arranging for certain rivals to be targeted by authorities. Specifically, the arrests of El Lobo and El Tigre, picked up by the army a few months apart of each other, seemed very convenient.

Several Milenio Cartel lieutenants outside the Valencia clan had their doubts about Mencho. One in particular, Ramiro Pozos González, alias "El Molca," had been a close friend of El Lobo prior to his arrest. He strongly believed that Mencho may have worked with Coronel to have the brothers removed. He refused to obey Mencho and founded his own splinter group named La Resistencia (The Resistance), while those affiliated with Mencho became known as Los Torcidos (The Twisted Ones).

In order to secure his place on the throne, Mencho travelled to Sinaloa to sit down with El Chapo with a very clear deal in mind. Mencho, ably seconded by his brother-in-law, Abigael Gonzalez Valencia, alias "El Cuini," would take over the meth and cocaine trafficking operations left behind by Coronel in Jalisco but remain loyal to the Sinaloa Cartel.

The name of his new group: the Jalisco Cartel New Generation (CJNG), with the title having first appeared on "narco-banners" (messages hung from bridges or pinned to walls) in the summer of 2010.

El Chapo agreed, and a war ensued between Mencho's loyalists and the renegade lieutenants known as La Resistencia. In an effort to gain an advantage in Michoacán, El Molca sought help from the worst enemies of the Milenio Cartel: the Zetas and the Familia Michoacana.

But the spread of the CJNG, backed by the support of the Sinaloa Cartel, proved too much and La Resistencia was overwhelmed. In September 2012, El Molca was arrested, which would take him out of the story, except that he gave a police interview in which he revealed extensive details about the Milenio Cartel.[18]

In the interview, a visibly exhausted González made two predictions. He said that Mencho would lead a "war without end" and that the Sinaloa Cartel and the CJNG would fight "the next war," engulfing neighbouring states like Michoacán and Zacatecas.

Twelve years on, El Molca's instincts have proven true. The two groups are indeed fighting an unending war, while Michoacán and Zacatecas are consistently among the most violent parts of the country.

The CJNG Coast-to-Coast

Mencho was quickly able to dominate much of the trafficking routes once controlled by the Milenio Cartel, but he was not satisfied. He knew that, to carve a real niche for itself, the CJNG had to expand rapidly.

In 2011, Mencho had already made advances into Colima, where the port of Manzanillo is located, and the central state of Guanajuato, a foreign investment hub north of Mexico City replete with heavy industry and oil pipelines.

Both of these advances were strategic. Being present at the port of Manzanillo gave the CJNG a major seaport from which to import cocaine from South America and chemical precursors for methamphetamine from China. This was a privilege the Valencia family had lost since being driven from Michoacán and losing access to the port of Lázaro Cárdenas.

Guanajuato offered up plentiful criminal profits. The state is ideally located in central Mexico, borders Jalisco and Michoacán, is close to Mexico City, and offers easy access to highways heading to the US Coast and the Atlantic Ocean. It also contains the vast Salamanca refinery, which allowed the CJNG to begin lucrative oil theft.

Both Colima and Guanajuato have remained crucial operating hubs for the CJNG for well over a decade. Around this time, Mencho set up two armed wings within the CJNG, both with leaderships he trusted. Grupo Delta would be tasked with being the muscle closer to home, operating in Jalisco and Michoacán, while Grupo Elite would oversee the newly conquered territory of Guanajuato and other states in central Mexico.

The next wave of expansion would come under the guise of the CJNG and the Sinaloa Cartel's campaign against the Zetas (see Matazetas chapter). In 2011, the CJNG hit back against their old enemies, which had driven them out of Michoacán. Their target: the state of Veracruz stretching up much of the Gulf of Mexico.

In September 2011, 35 alleged Zeta members were found dead under a bridge in the state capital of Veracruz. Within a couple of weeks, 32 more people were killed in two properties in the city.

Targeting Veracruz served two clear purposes.

First, it disrupted the Zetas' drug trafficking corridor along Mexico's eastern coastline from the Yucatan peninsula up to Nuevo Laredo, according to Stratfor, a strategic intelligence company.[19] Taking the fight to the Zetas in Veracruz essentially helped to, at least to a small extent, disrupt their drug trafficking supply line.

Second, it gave the CJNG a foothold on both coastlines. To project force into Veracruz, the CJNG could build on strong foundations along the Pacific Coast and in central Mexico.

The next major hurdle came in April 2012 when Erick Valencia Salazar, alias "El 85," was arrested in Guadalajara. Valencia Salazar had held immense power and influence within the Milenio Cartel and had helped keep the family united since the arrests of El Lobo and El Tigre. He had also been an important supporter of Mencho's bid for leadership.[20]

Valencia Salazar is believed to have been involved in every early success by the CJNG, whether it was winning the civil war against La Resistencia, planning the Matazetas attacks or firming up the CJNG's reception of chemical precursors through the port of Manzanillo. When the Milenio Cartel was working under the Sinaloa Cartel, Valencia Salazar had worked to import large quantities of ephedrine and other precursors through Manzanillo, a business he continued for the CJNG.[21]

Valencia Salazar was arrested during an army raid in Zapopan, Jalisco, and the CJNG responded with a show of strength. In response, the cartel burned dozens of vehicles across Jalisco's capital of Guadalajara, especially public buses. In a mildly humorous twist, the CJNG would then put up banners apologizing for the rioting, saying it had been due to an outpouring of emotion for Valencia Salazar, and that the group would now return to killing Zetas.

His removal, however, confirmed Mencho as the sole leader within the CJNG. Again, Mencho's involvement in the raid that nabbed El 85 has been the subject of much speculation. A New Yorker profile speculated the real target had been Mencho, while other reports alleged Mencho provided information to authorities that led to Valencia Salazar's arrest.[22]

El 85 believed Mencho was responsible for his capture. And upon being released from prison in 2018, he helped create a rival group to attack the CJNG. (see chapter on the CJNG's Many, Many Wars).

It's Time to Go Home

With Mencho's leadership status confirmed, the Zetas on the back foot, and the CJNG settled on both coasts, the group moved to reclaim its homeland. In 2012 and 2013, the CJNG would make progressively larger incursions back into Michoacán.

At the time, the power in Michoacán lay with the Caballeros Templarios (Knights Templar). Originally a faction of Carlos Rosales' La Familia Michoacana, the Knights Templar had become a powerful criminal group, mostly from controlling the vast production of methamphetamine.[23]

Removing them from Michoacán was crucial to the CJNG's planned takeover of the state. Yet it would not be easy. The Knights Templar had their hooks deep into Michoacán's political and security apparatus. In 2014, the governor of Michoacán, Fausto Vallejo, was forced to resign after his son appeared in a photo with leaders of the Knights Templar. Vallejo's interior secretary, Jose de Jesus Reyna García, was jailed that same year for ties to the group.

But meanwhile, the group was committing atrocities in Michoacán. Extortion, theft and beatings were commonplace in communities controlled by the Knights Templar, and locals fought back.

A wave of community defence groups, known as auto-defensas, sprang up gradually across Michoacán to fight back the Knights Templar. The CJNG made a convenient bedfellow for these migrants. The Milenio Cartel, especially the Valencia family, were remembered for the ways it provided jobs and supported locals in times of need.[25]

The CJNG allied with a number of auto-defensas groups to begin pushing the Knights Templar out of crucial parts of Michoacán with access to the Pacific Coast and connections to the ports of Lázaro Cárdenas and Manzanillo.

Much has been written about the nature of Michoacán's self-defense groups and whether they should be referred to as vigilantes, community guards, or criminal groups of their own. The truth is likely a blend of all three.

For example, one of the CJNG's main allies in their campaign against the Knights Templar was Juan José Farias Alvarez, alias "El Abuelo" (The Grandfather). In 2013, El Abuelo founded a self-defence group and sought to paint himself as a defender of his hometown of Tepalcatepec in Michoacán. In truth, El Abuelo was a veteran drug trafficker and opportunist who had worked at different times for the Valencias and La Familia Michoacana. He switched allegiances again to the CJNG when the time was right.[26]

In Michoacán, the CJNG also began deploying a "divide and conquer" approach. This strategy was described as "against the Zetas, the CJNG offered its matazetas. Faced with the Templars, they framed themselves as matatemplarios (Templar Killers)" by Mexican investigator Jesús Pérez Caballero.[27]

The war in Michoacán between the CJNG and the Knights Templar only further associated Mencho's group with the worst horrors in the country. Bodies hanging from bridges or decapitated heads with messages left next to them became commonplace as the CJNG slowly gained the edge.

In 2014 and 2015, the Knights Templar would be decapitated, with the killing of one leader, Nazario Moreno, alias "El Chayo," and the arrest of another, Servando Gómez Martínez, alias "La Tuta."

The self-defense groups had succeeded in their mission, backed by the CJNG. But peace would not last for long as the CJNG sought to establish the same hegemony as the Knights Templar. Its former allies would soon become sworn enemies.

The CJNG had come home but in bitter circumstances.

THE CJNG'S MANY, MANY WARS

The CJNG was linked to 81% of all deaths involving cartel violence in Mexico from 2013 to 2022, according to data from the Uppsala Conflict Data Program collated in Mexico's Peace Index 2023.[1]

This statistic encapsulates the tens of thousands of people who have been killed or have disappeared, and the hundreds of thousands more who have lost loved ones. It also does not include the many more casualties the CJNG has been complicit in killing, including tens of thousands of opioid overdose victims.

Yet, what has the CJNG achieved through all this slaughter? It has become one of the two most powerful cartels in the country and raked in billions of dollars in profits. But its wars have not led to many significant or permanent victories. There are few parts of Mexico where the CJNG does not still face some sort of rival.

The concepts of "victory" and "defeat" are often unhelpful when discussing Mexico's warring cartels. The very nature of these criminal networks rarely makes their "defeat" complete. Certain once-powerful criminal networks, such as the Guadalajara Cartel or the Zetas, no longer exist because their top leaders were killed or arrested, and their membership dissipated.

But many of these members brought their knowledge of drug trafficking routes, money laundering, meth and fentanyl production, extortion or assassination to other groups.

Drug trafficking is a legacy business. Like a corporate rebranding for a bankrupt company, traffickers can reappear under a different name.

The CJNG is evidence of this. Its criminal forebears were known as the Avocado Kings. The Milenio Cartel. The Matazetas. The Torcidos. The Cuinis. Then the CJNG.

But once it firmly settled on its four-letter identity, the CJNG has sought "victory" over all comers. Its expansion model is very similar to that pioneered by its former nemesis, the Zetas.

The CJNG expands like a virus. When it commits to a new area in Mexico, it seeks to take over all potential avenues of criminal profit. Specific local rackets, such as illegal fishing, illegal mining, oil theft, hotel extortion, are incorporated. Existing gangs may be co-opted into the CJNG, acting in its name but retaining a measure of independence. Or they may be removed. Larger rivals are warned to cease their activities, with leaders targeted by name on narco-banners or in propaganda videos, and then brutally attacked.

For over a decade, the CJNG has been highly successful at taking over new territory from its competition.

But it has also failed to become Mexico's dominant criminal actor. Such a title is impossible to achieve, let alone hold.

As this list will show, the CJNG has found it difficult to establish its hegemony in much of the country. It has faced dogged resistance from national-level rivals and smaller, entrenched groups, as well as interventions by Mexico's police, army and National Guard.

This list does not break down every variation, sub-group and named faction that the CJNG has come up against. But in looking at the CJNG's major battles since 2020, it shows the truth of Mexico's drug wars.

There's always someone left to fight.

Alemanes (*San Luis Potosí*)

Mexico's federal Highway 57 winds its way for almost 1,300 kilometres from Mexico City to the US border across eight states. One stretch of this road going through the northern state of San Luis Potosí has proven to be a lucrative windfall for the Alemanes. Cargo theft, drug trafficking and kidnapping, the highway brought a steady flow of victims and opportunities.

Yet another group created by Zeta exiles, the Alemanes have also become serial kidnappers of migrants seeking to reach the US. In April 2023, a group of 23 people disappeared along Highway 57 near the town of Matehuala, an Alemanes stronghold.[2]

In investigating this disappearance, investigators eventually rescued 106 people kidnapped, with suspicion rapidly falling on the Alemanes.

The Alemanes have tried repeatedly to defend their territory from CJNG incursions since at least 2020. In 2022, a CJNG affiliate in San Luis Potosí, identifying itself as Operacion Bélica, announced it would "clean out the area of rats" in a video directly threatening the Alemanes and its leaders.[3]

Since then, the conflict has continued to simmer but the Alemanes have received little attention, outside of the mass kidnapping of migrants.

Cartel del Abuelo (*Michoacán*)

The Cartel del Abuelo, also known as the Cartel de Tepalcatepec, is a self-defence group turned criminal organisation in the state of Michoacán, Mexico. Led by Juan José Farías Álvarez, alias "El Abuelo" (The Grandfather), the group began as a supporter of the CJNG. Farias had been a drug trafficker associated with the Valencia family in the days of the Milenio Cartel, before making a stand against the Knights Templar in 2013 and 2014. His local self-defence group initially worked with the CJNG.[4]

But following the fall of the Knights Templar, the CJNG offended its smaller, local allies as it sought to dominate Michoacán's criminal landscape. Farias' hometown of Tepalcatepec is a drug trafficking hotspot as it has easy road connections to the ports of Lázaro Cárdenas and Manzanillo, as well as Acapulco to the south.[5]

Farias became a bitter foe of the CJNG and joined the Cárteles Unidos, a coalition of Michoacán groups fighting to defend their turf, from the larger group.6 The Cartel del Abuelo has fought the CJNG intensely since 2019 and is heavily involved in methamphetamine production and distribution.

Cartel Mafia Veracruzana (*Veracruz*)

There are always seemingly new players in the criminal landscape of northern Veracruz. Splinter groups from the Zetas, various factions from the Gulf Cartel, and local gangs have all made themselves heard. But one group that has stood out from the pack is the Cartel Mafia Veracruzana (CMV), also known as Grupo Sombra.[7]

Grupo Sombra originally split off from the Gulf Cartel before setting itself up as the CMV. It has been feuding independently with the CJNG to control towns such as Poza Rica and Tuxpan and territory north towards the Tamaulipas border.

Their fight with the CJNG has been ongoing since at least 2019 but appears to have escalated in 2024. The remains of at least 15 bodies were found in two vehicles on a bridge in Tuxpan in January 2024, with a threatening message from the CJNG targeted at the "Sombras."[8] Days later, the CMV responded with a series of narco-banners of their own. Then, in March, CMV members were filmed dumping the dismembered remains of several bodies in broad daylight on a square in a small town near Poza Rica.[9]

The ability of the CMV to fight off the CJNG in a prolonged campaign is unknown, but the group may have also allied itself with Los Tercios, another Veracruz outfit that has clashed with the CJNG.

Cárteles Unidos (*Michoacán*)

The Cárteles Unidos (CU) is an alliance formed to combat the incursion of the powerful Jalisco New Generation Cartel (CJNG) into the Mexican state of Michoacán. It brings together various local criminal groups like the Cartel de Tepalcatepec, the Viagras and remnants of the Familia Michoacana and Knights Templar groups.[10]

This reads like a laundry list of former CJNG allies and enemies. Around 2013 and 2014, when seeking to gain an edge against the Knights Templar in Michoacán, the CJNG made deals with vigilante self-defence groups such as that run by Juan José Farías Álvarez, alias "El Abuelo."

But once the Knights Templar were ousted, distrust at the CJNG grew as the group sought to dominate Michoacán's lucrative drug trafficking routes, synthetic drug production across the Tierra Caliente region, the profitable extortion of avocado farmers, and control for some of the state's gold, silver and iron mines.

This prompted the different groups to unite into the Cárteles Unidos alliance to protect their stake in 2019. Since then, the CU and CJNG have been locked in a bloody conflict to control this territory. The violence has been particularly intense around CU strongholds like Tepalcatepec, Aguililla and Buenavista.[11]

The turf war has seen both sides employ tactics like blockades, cutting off towns from the outside world, and hanging bodies from bridges.[12]

The war against the CU has been one of the most absurdly wasteful in Mexico's horrific drug war. Thousands have been killed in a violent slog that has seen the CJNG and CU continue to commit to control Michoacán's criminal real estate, corrupting or killing politicians, and displacing entire communities.

Yet the dynamics have hardly changed. Predictable interventions from security forces have punctuated any territorial gains by the CJNG or any pushback by the CU. The battles for Aguililla from 2019 to 2022 have been a dizzying and confusing example of just how violent but stagnant Michoacán's dynamics really are.[13]

Aguililla is the founding place of the Milenio Cartel and the closest town to Mencho's birthplace.

In October 2019, a large police convoy was driving through the town when CJNG gunmen ambushed it. Thirteen officers were killed and three more were injured.[14]

In April, amid a renewed besieging of the town in which hundreds were displaced, the CJNG ambushed a camp belonging to the Viagras and slaughtered an unconfirmed number of men, with estimates ranging between 12 and 18.

In response, the CU put barricades up around the entire city, corralling residents in and making it difficult for food and medical supplies to enter. The situation got progressively worse over the next year, with the level of violence and deprivation verging on a "humanitarian crisis," according to Falko Ernst, a leading researcher on conflict in Michoacán.[15] In 2021, the Catholic Church even got involved with the Vatican's ambassador to Mexico visiting Aguililla in April to call for peace.[16]

In April 2021, the CJNG celebrated finally taking over control of the town, only for the Mexican army to state the group had reportedly been driven out by a strong military intervention in February 2022.[17] This exile doesn't appear to have lasted long as within a month, the mayor of Aguililla and his political advisor were both killed by the CJNG.[18]

This back-and-forth state of affairs has remained in place until early 2024. Michoacán, as a whole, has seen violence drop progressively since early 2023 but remains among the most violent states in Mexico.

The CJNG-CU war also had a broader impact on Mexico's criminal dynamics: the beginning of drone warfare.

In the summer of 2020, the CJNG began strapping C4 explosives to readily available civilian drones and using them to terrorize CU opponents around Tepalcatepec. This was the start of numerous such deployments of drones, including some that have dropped homemade bombs onto enemies.[19]

Their use soon spread. In 2023, hundreds of residents were reported as fleeing from the southern state of Guerrero due to drones connected to the CJNG. At first, the drones seemed to mostly have a terror effect, but were not highly effective at actually killing their targets.

But the CJNG persevered. A unit of drone pilots is known to wear a Droneros patch on their uniforms. And in February 2024, at least four soldiers were killed and nine others injured during an ambush in Michoacán, which involved explosive drones.[20]

Correa (*Michoacán*)

The Correa clan are one of the newer players in Michoacán's busy criminal scene. Based in the state's northern mountain areas, the Correa were mostly associated with illegal logging before expanding into marijuana production and synthetic drugs. In 2021 and 2022, several massacres were connected to this feud. Most notably, the Correa were allegedly responsible for killing 20 people at a ranch, including "El Barbas," one of the CJNG's leaders in Michoacán.[21]

Led by Daniel Correa, alias "El Tigre," the Correa has proven to be a small but well-entrenched thorn in the CJNG's side. This has allowed the group to actually grow its size and capacity, allegedly receiving support from other CJNG enemies such as La Familia Michoacana.

Gulf Cartel (*Tamaulipas, Veracruz*)

The Gulf Cartel has been through several incarnations. The Gulf Cartel of 2024, splintering into warring fronts that spend as much time fighting each other as their traditional enemies, is a far cry from the rampaging Gulf Cartel of 2003. Led by Osiel Cárdenas Guillén, the Gulf Cartel ran Tamaulipas with an iron hand and sent the Zetas rampaging into Michoacán, forcing the Milenio Cartel into exile *(see chapter on the CJNG's Origins)*.

It was that exile which led to the creation of the CJNG and twenty years later, the tables have turned. The CJNG have turned up in Tamaulipas and have got the Gulf Cartel rattled. In May 2023, reports from Tamaulipas stated that the CJNG was making a play to take the three important border cities of Reynosa, Matamoros and perhaps even Nuevo Laredo.[22] Since these are important crossing points into the US, the criminal advantages for the CJNG are obvious. Fighting has been particularly intense in the municipality of San Fernando Valley, important for its highway connections to two border crossings.

And the Gulf Cartel may be hard-pressed to resist. Different units within it, originally founded to protect certain cities, have gone into business for themselves, such as the Panthers in Nuevo Laredo, the Cyclones and the Scorpions in Matamoros and the Metros in Reynosa. Each is responding differently to the CJNG, with the Metros allegedly having struck up a lasting alliance with the four-letter group.[23]

La Familia Michoacana (*Michoacán*)

This one is complicated. The name of La Familia Michoacana (LFM) has been used for decades in Michoacán and is intricately tied to violence in the state and the evolution of the CJNG. It was first used in the 1980s by Carlos Rosales Mendoza, alias "Tísico," a marijuana trafficker with ambitions of grandeur, according to the DEA.[24] There are longstanding allegations that the group also acted as vigilantes to prevent other forms of local crime.

As Michoacán became a focal point of the Mexican drug trade in the late 1990s, Rosales became a tentative ally of the Valencia family. He helped the family make drug trafficking connections to the Gulf Cartel in Tamaulipas, run by Rosales' close friend, Osiel Cárdenas Guillén. An unhappy love triangle led to the shattering of this alliance *(see chapter on the CJNG's Origins)*.

LFM allied themselves with the Zetas, the Gulf Cartel's enforcers at the time, and drove the Valencias out of the state.[25] The group used this momentum to take over drug trafficking in Michoacán, producing marijuana and heroin, setting up meth labs, and importing cocaine through the port of Lázaro Cardenas.

After Rosales was arrested in 2004, a new generation of leaders expanded the group further and added a religious component to it. Despite openly engaging in a range of criminal economies, LFM would claim to be acting with divine justice.

The cartel expanded so rapidly and violently that it became a major priority for both Mexican and US authorities. Sustained operations against its leadership and drug trafficking networks led LFM to lose momentum in the late 2000s. In 2010, a major internal split led to a good part of LFM's membership leaving to form the Knights Templar) and claiming much of LFM's territory.[26]

While the cartel was severely weakened, the name hung around. From 2011 to 2014, as the CJNG progressively sought to drive the Knights Templar out of Michoacán, it recruited a coalition of local support, including former LFM members.

By 2015, however, the CJNG's ambition of dominating Michoacán had become evident, and its allies turned against it, including LFM.[27]

Since then, the LFM situation has become blurry. LFM has been rebuilt in the last decade and is again a powerful force on the Mexican criminal landscape. As of 2024, it was controlled by two brothers, José Alfredo Olascoaga Hurtado, alias "El Fresa," and Johnny Olascoaga Hurtado, alias "El Pez." Both are among the most wanted criminals in Mexico.[28]

But despite keeping its name and a presence in its original home state, LFM has carved out a criminal niche in the neighbouring State of Mexico and Guerrero.

Its relations with the CJNG have been tumultuous and difficult to clarify, as is standard for Michoacán. In April 2022, the Correa, a small criminal group from the north of the state, killed at least 20 people at an underground cockfight organized by the CJNG. Observers at the time believed Pez and Fresa may have ordered the massacre.[29]

But by early 2023, a partial alliance between LFM and the CJNG was apparently in effect, with LFM members even being trained to use the CJNG's drone warfare against enemies in Guerrero.[30]

And just to add a layer of confusion, the name *La Nueva Familia Michoacana* has also appeared prominently in both narco-banners as well as official security reports. This has led to widespread confusion as to if this is a wholly different group. However, the name may only have been in use for a short time as a way to distinguish the revival of LFM but does not refer to a separate faction.[31]

More twists in this tale can be expected.

Mezcales (*Colima*)

In 2022, Colima was the deadliest state in all of Mexico. It reached an absolutely staggering 110 murders per 100,000 people, the highest level for any single Mexican state since records began.[32]

A major contributing factor to this grim record came after a small group known as the Mezcales began contesting the CJNG's control of the port of Manzanillo.

Part of the sustained violence in a state considered to be part of the CJNG's heartland has been the breakdown in relations between the powerful cartel and one of its smaller factions, Los Mezcales. José Bernabé Brizuela Meraz, alias "La Vaca" (The Cow), was an experienced drug trafficker having worked for a number of criminal groups, including the Tijuana and Juárez cartels, before eventually settling in with the CJNG.[33]

He became an important operator for the four-letter group in the state of Colima, but gradually began seeking his independence. In 2019 and 2020, he built up the Mezcales.[34]

The group remained as a seemingly loyal part of the CJNG but tensions had clearly been boiling. In early 2022, two events shattered what was left of their alliance.

In January of that year, a riot at a prison in Colima left twelve people dead, allegedly after a fight between members of both sides. In February, a narco-banner stated that La Vaca had refused to obey a CJNG order to assassinate the state governor of Colima.[35] Amid copious insults and colourful language, La Vaca signed the banner as the Cartel Independiente de Colima (Independent Colima Cartel). He was quite literally declaring independence.

Within a few days, more banners went up. This time, they bore severe news, alleging that Mencho had allegedly suffered a cardiac arrest and died, leading La Vaca to leave the CJNG. "I owe respect and loyalty only to Mencho," wrote the Mezcales boss.[36]

The CJNG took this threat seriously. Hundreds of deaths were linked to the broader CJNG-Mezcales feud. The state capital, also called Colima, saw murders almost double year-on-year, becoming the most violent city in the world, according to one study.[37]

However, the Mezcales were almost immediately on the back foot. Colima has been one of the CJNG's main bases, due to the presence of the port of Manzanillo and a synthetic drug production empire, for over a decade.

La Vaca was arrested in Mexico City in August 2022, while his right-hand man, known as El Cejon, was detained days later carrying thousands of fentanyl pills. Another top leader was arrested in June 2023. The group has limped on since under the command of La Vaca's sister, Blanca Elizabeth Brizuela Meraz, alias "La Paloma" (The Dove).[38]

Northeast Cartel (*Tamaulipas*)

The Cartel del Noreste (Northeast Cartel) holds onto the border city of Nuevo Laredo with an iron grip. Graffiti of its three leaders, CDN, are displayed across the city.[39]

Nuevo Laredo, sitting across the Rio Grande from Laredo, Texas, is worth defending. It is a criminal cash cow. Millions of dollars in cocaine, fentanyl and meth pass through the city every year going north. American-made guns flow south into Mexico.

But as Mexico's migration crisis has grown particularly acute and thousands wait for their US asylum appointments, the Northeast Cartel is preying on them non-stop. Kidnappings, extortion, and other forms of violence against migrants have skyrocketed across the state.[40]

In Nuevo Laredo, kidnappings have become so common that they are casually referred to as "passing through the office." Families are dragged out of their tents at camps and entire buses of migrants are taken. Police officers even "sell" migrants to criminals.[41]

The CJNG wants a piece of the action. Since 2019, they have fought the Northeast Cartel to try and break its stranglehold on Nuevo Laredo and highways leading there. The group has made some inroads into the city. Authorities have blamed the CJNG for being partially responsible for the 200% increase in the amount of methamphetamine found in Nuevo Laredo from 2022 and 2023.[42]

But the CJNG has not come close to dislodging the Northeast Cartel. The arrest of Northeast Cartel leader Juan Gerardo Treviño, alias "El Huevo" (The Egg), in March 2022 could have been a turning point. The Mexican government called it one of the major arrests of the decade and the group responded with a show of force.[43]

But two years on, the Northeast Cartel continues to rule Nuevo Laredo. And in terms of murders, the city and indeed the whole of Tamaulipas have been relatively peaceful. February 2024 saw the lowest number of monthly murders in the state for a decade.[44] And instead of the CJNG moving in, the Northeast Cartel appears to be expanding south into Nuevo León.

Nueva Plaza (Jalisco)

The CJNG has remained remarkably united, even with the rumors swirling about Mencho's alleged death.

But there are some noteworthy exceptions. Nueva Plaza may be the foremost among these.

In August 2017, Marcos Hernández, a high-ranking CJNG financial operator, was shot dead while driving his red and black BMW i8 in Zapopan, Jalisco. The murder was quickly pinned on Carlos Enrique Sánchez Martínez, alias "El Cholo," a close lieutenant to Mencho. Some media reports state El Cholo had been planning his betrayal for a while, while others say he killed Hernández after the latter found out El Cholo was stealing money from the CJNG.[45]

Either way, the murder marked El Cholo's split from the CJNG and he founded Nueva Plaza, a group which looked to take over the control of several key towns in Jalisco, especially around its capital, Guadalajara. Nueva Plaza gained a great boost when it was joined by Erick Valencia Salazar, alias "El 85."[46]

A Valencia turning on the CJNG was virtually unheard of. El 85 had been a close ally to Mencho but was captured in 2012. Speculation has been rife that Mencho may have sold Valencia Salazar out to authorities to remove a potential rival.

Low-ranking members of the CJNG may have jumped ship at the idea of gaining more power and influence in a newer group. But despite operating inside the CJNG's home turf of Jalisco, Nueva Plaza has never really taken off as a real threat, despite alleged connections to the Sinaloa Cartel.[47]

Localized violence has happened in and around Guadalajara, but Nueva Plaza has gone quiet. El Cholo was captured, gruesomely tortured, and killed by the CJNG in 2021. The video in which he confessed his betrayal before his execution has been widely circulated.[48]

Santa Rosa de Lima Cartel (*Guanajuato*)

"Whenever you want, New Generation Cartel, we're here waiting for you. What are you waiting for, assholes?"

This was the bold cry with which the Santa Rosa de Lima Cartel (SRLC) declared war on the CJNG in a video released in October 2017.[49] Its leader, José Antonio Yépez Ortíz, alias "El Marro" (The Sledgehammer), is flanked by dozens of heavily armed men in a show of force.

Crude defiance notwithstanding, this fight should have been over in the first round.

On one side, the all-powerful CJNG, with thousands of well-armed members, bankrolled by a sprawling drug trafficking empire. On the other, a ragtag group of fuel thieves from central Guanajuato, united to resist a larger conquering force.

More than six years on, the fight has lasted longer than the Second World War, the SRLC has been battered but not beaten, and Guanajuato is one of the deadliest places in the world.[50]

This battle was not fought for drugs but for fuel. Guanajuato is home to the large Salamanca refinery and its interconnected network of pipelines. Prior to 2017, the SRLC existed as a group dedicated to fuel theft headquartered in the town of Santa Rosa de Lima, about 80 kilometres north of the Salamanca refinery.[51]

The CJNG took notice of these potential profits and moved in. In response, the SRLC united various bands of fuel thieves, leading to the 2017 video.[52]

The SRLC proved a tough nut to crack and, by 2018, Guanajuato was already the most violent state in Mexico with over 3,500 murders in one year.

In 2019, President Andrés Manuel López Obrador made fighting fuel theft a security priority and sent troops to Guanajuato to quell the violence.[53]

In response, El Marro left a narco-banner near the Salamanca refinery, telling the president to remove all soldiers or innocent people would die.[54]

El Marro also responded brutally to anyone suspected of collaborating with the CJNG and authorities. Following the arrest of his mother, sister, and cousin in June 2020, gunmen entered a drug rehabilitation facility in Irapuato and shot dead 27 people, with authorities rapidly blaming the SRLC.[55]

In August 2020, El Marro was arrested. But any celebration by the CJNG was short-lived. The SRLC was weakened by its leader being detained, but it has proved highly resilient.[56]

One reason is that it has continued to expand from being a fuel theft gang into being a far more diverse criminal group. Through extortion, drug trafficking and kidnapping, the SRLC has broadened its sources of income, allowing it to better finance its campaign against the CJNG.

Another is that El Marro and his family continue to inspire tremendous loyalty. According to police reports, the SRLC is now controlled by El Marro's sister, Karen Lizbeth.

Sinaloa Cartel (*Nationwide*)

In September 2012, Mexican police arrested Ramiro Pozos González, alias "El Molca." A veteran of Jalisco's criminal scene, El Molca made a prediction in his police interview. He warned that the next drug war to shake Mexico would involve the Sinaloa Cartel, already a criminal heavyweight, and the CJNG, still in its infancy at the time.[57]

El Molca knew what he was talking about. He had worked for the Milenio Cartel during its alliance with the Sinaloa Cartel and had fought against Mencho's attempted takeover and rebranding of the group as the CJNG.

It would take a few years for his prediction to come true. The historical connecting tissue that tied the Sinaloa Cartel to the CJNG would be preserved for a few years.

But by 2015, this tissue had frayed, and the two groups were on a collision course. The rampaging Zetas had been broken. The power of the Gulf Cartel was curtailed and contained to a section of the US border.

The Sinaloa Cartel and the CJNG were the only cartels with a national presence. Their war has been a constant driver of violence in Mexico over the last eight years. The World of Crime focuses on three specific areas within this conflict to illustrate its scope:

Tijuana

One of the first flashpoints was in Tijuana, a border city of more than 2 million people, where the Sinaloa Cartel had maintained a strong level of control. The CJNG made their presence felt in Tijuana, battling to control both drug trafficking corridors to the United States.[58]

Homicides jumped by 80% year-on-year in 2015 and the CJNG also made an alliance with the remnants of the Tijuana Cartel to make it the Tijuana Cartel New Generation (CTNG).

The majority of drugs entering the US from Mexico cross through or nearby Tijuana, the CJNG's arrival also coincided with confusion within the Sinaloa Cartel after the January 2016 recapture of its kingpin, Joaquín Guzmán Loera, alias "El Chapo."[59]

Over the next eight years, Tijuana's importance has only been enhanced by the surge in demand for fentanyl. Around 60% of all fentanyl seized in the US in that time entered via Southern California border crossings, according to authorities in San Diego.[60]

But Tijuana offered drug trafficking profits beyond what could be sent to the United States. The CJNG has fought years of brutal battles against Sinaloa Cartel envoys to control the local trafficking sales in the city.

Most of those killed or arrested were low-level drug dealers or gunmen sent in by more powerful paymasters. Tijuana broke its homicide record with over 1,700 murders in 2017. That rose to 2,200 by 2019, with only a small drop since.

But the local community has also been affected. Meth and heroin, then fentanyl, Tijuana's addicts have been battered by the range of drugs being moved through their city.[61]

In 2023, the city was still a criminal free-for-all. While Mexican police reports stated the Sinaloa Cartel remained the strongest group in Tijuana, violence has remained high with a CJNG faction known as Los Cabos blamed for some of the worst of it.[62]

Zacatecas

The Sinaloa Cartel and the CJNG fight bitterly for control of Zacatecas. The state is right in the centre of Mexico and sits on several highways connecting to the US border. In other words, it is the perfect place to transport and stock large shipments of drugs. In turn, these easy logistics have made Zacatecas a fentanyl production hotspot, with several large facilities dismantled in the centre and south of the state.[63]

From 2019, the CJNG and Sinaloa Cartel clashed regularly in the state. A brutal riot at the Cereso prison in the town of Cieneguillas left at least 17 prisoners dead on both sides.

But in 2020, the CJNG fully committed to removing the Sinaloa Cartel and other rivals from Zacatecas. In April, CJNG narco-banners went up in 17 towns and cities, all promising to rid the state of kidnappings and extortion.[64]

Over the next two years, murders, including repeated brutal massacres of Sinaloa and CJNG members, soared. Zacatecas broke its homicide records, topping out at 1,134 murders in 2021. In response, the government launched Operation Zacatecas 2, with almost 4,000 army and National Guard troops sent to pacify the situation.[65]

While homicide numbers have gone down slightly since, Zacatecas saw the third-most massacres, events in which more than one person was killed, in all of Mexico in 2023.

The state's sheer importance and the amount of resources both sides are committing to fighting for it make it unlikely a winner will emerge in Zacatecas anytime soon.

Chiapas

Despite being one of the main places for cocaine, weapons, and migrants entering Mexico, and with all the criminal opportunities these bring, Chiapas managed to stay relatively peaceful. The Sinaloa Cartel had a heavy presence along its Mexico-Guatemala border, which went largely uncontested.

Until the CJNG caught on to the advantages, not only of controlling Chiapas, but of operating in Guatemala as well. Since 2022, the state has become one of Mexico's main Sinaloa-CJNG battlegrounds, leading to tens of thousands being displaced.[66]

The violence has been particularly intense around the border town of Frontera Comalapa. Local residents have confirmed that the increase in homicides has been largely connected to the CJNG, who are accused of trying to forcibly recruit people into fighting the Sinaloa Cartel. An alliance between the larger cartel and a local paramilitary group, known as Maiz, has only further increased the violence.[67]

Securing the border area would be highly useful to the CJNG's operations in Guatemala, where it has made alliances with Guatemalan drug traffickers to smuggle cocaine, heroin, and meth into Mexico.

Talibanes (*Zacatecas*)

The Talibanes are not named for any direct connections to the Afghan terror group. Instead, their founder, Iván Velázquez Caballero, was known as "El Taliban" for his habit of decapitating his enemies with machetes.[68]

Velázquez Caballero was sent by the Zetas to head their operations in Zacatecas around 2007 and quickly became a figure of terror in the state, according to a Sin Embargo investigation.[69]

He seems to have taken quite a liking to his surroundings, as when the Zetas sought to replace him in 2011, he rebelled.

Although Velázquez Caballero was arrested in 2012 and subsequently extradited to the US, his Talibanes remained a quiet fixture in Zacatecas' criminal underworld. They remained under the radar but operated in northern Zacatecas and along its border with San Luis Potosí, focusing on local drug sales, extortion and the theft of everything from cars to cattle.

Over the years, they gained a reputation as being the absolute masters of this corner of Mexico, cowing mayors and police commanders.[70]

Since 2021, the Talibanes have been one of the main drivers in the violence which has consumed large parts of Zacatecas, especially in the north of the state. While much of this fighting has pitted the CJNG against the Sinaloa Cartel, the Talibanes have often been described as allies helping the Sinaloa Cartel.[71]

Zetas Vieja Escuela (*Tamaulipas, Veracruz*)

Upon the splintering of the Zetas in the early 2010s, the Zetas Vieja Escuela (Old School Zetas) sought to cast themselves as the true successors of the brutal paramilitary group.

Headquartered in the Zetas' main strongholds in Veracruz, Tamaulipas and Nuevo León, the Old School Zetas fought a bitter and brutal campaign to try and prevent the expansion of the CJNG in these states starting in 2016.[72]

This proved particularly brutal in the state of Veracruz, with a series of tit-for-tat executions and massacres. In April 2019, days after the Old School Zetas tortured and killed three alleged CJNG members, CJNG hitmen burst into a birthday party in the town of Minatitlán.[73]

Since then, its rivalry with the CJNG has quietened. The Zetas Vieja Escuela have seemingly become more focused on a battle involving several offshoots of the Zetas and the Gulf Cartel for control of Tamaulipas.[74]

THE MATAZETAS

Certain criminal groups have etched their legacy in Mexico's history forever. This should not be taken as praise. These legacies were written in blood.

Of all the many groups to have populated Mexico's criminal map, the Sinaloa Cartel may have been the first to become a household name around the world, helped in large part by El Chapo's mainstream celebrity status.

The CJNG may not be quite so well-known around the world but are well on its way to becoming so. Its carefully rehearsed communication campaigns, its brutality, its economic diversification, even the debate about whether Mencho is still alive. All these factors have contributed to the legend of the CJNG.

But one facet of the group's history lives on more than 15 years after it began: the Matazetas.

The Origin of the Zetas

The Guadalajara Cartel, the Tijuana Cartel, the Gulf Cartel, the Beltrán-Leyva Organization were all powerful and transnational criminal threats that contributed to the drug crisis and security breakdown in Mexico.

But perhaps none of them are as famous as the brutal, militaristic and unhinged Zetas. From the late 1990s to the mid-2010s, the Zetas were behind some of the worst excesses of the Mexican drug war. This period would normalize the barbaric tactics that have most defined this violent period in Mexican history.

Yet, from 2009 onwards, a small group, whose actions remain largely mysterious, began to defy them. This group called itself the Matazetas (Zeta Killers), a name that remains attached to the CJNG.

But first, a brief history lesson.

The Zetas were born from the alliance of two men, Arturo Guzmán Decena and Osiel Cárdenas Guillén.

Guzmán Decena joined the Mexican army after school and rapidly joined the GAFE, a group of special forces commandos trained to fight severe internal threats. Guzmán Decena soon showed how he would go about fighting such threats.

In 1994, alarmed by decades of perceived government encroachment, loss of lands and abuse of natural resources, members of a number of indigenous communities in the southern state of Chiapas rose up. The Zapatista Army of National Liberation (EZLN) attacked a number of towns across Chiapas, freeing prisoners from jails, destroying land records, and took over government buildings.[2]

The Mexican government responded brutally to crush the uprising and over 150 Zapatista members and civilians were killed. At the centre of these killings were Guzmán Decena and the GAFE. In the small town of Ocosingo, 34 Zapatistas were found dead, their corpses in a heap. The next day, three more, their ears and noses sliced off.[3]

Guzmán Decena was then transferred north to Miguel Alemán, a city in the Mexican state of Tamaulipas right on the US border. The city was part of the territory of the Gulf Cartel, one of Mexico's longest-lasting and most powerful criminal groups.

In the late 1990s, the Gulf Cartel was facing a crisis of leadership. To secure the group permanently and bump off his rivals, Cárdenas Guillén was introduced to Guzmán Decena for help. It was a perfect arrangement. The GAFE man could offer unparalleled military skills and contacts, and the cartel boss could offer money, power and influence.

The brutality and cunning that the two deployed is perhaps best exemplified with a betrayal that seems ripped from a Mafia movie. In 1999, Cárdenas Guillén invited his Gulf Cartel rival, Salvador Gómez Herrera, to be his daughter's godfather. The two men got into a car where Guzmán Decena was waiting. As they drove, the special forces commando fired a bullet into the back of Gómez Herrera's head.

For this, Cárdenas Guillén became known as the Mata Amigo (Friend Killer) and the partnership was sealed.

Guzmán Decena reached out to his old GAFE buddies, offering them a different and lavish lifestyle. Many took him up on his offer and the Zetas quickly grew to a unit of about 40 military men, each identified by a code. Guzmán Decena, as their leader, was "Z-1."

Cárdenas Guillén, who was the Gulf Cartel's clear leader, deployed them as a brutal hit squad in and around Tamaulipas and beyond.

Cárdenas Guillén soon got into a bitter feud with Milenio Cartel, his former drug trafficking partners, in Michoacán *(see chapter on the CJNG's Origins)*. With an eye to securing control of the marijuana and opium poppy that had made the Milenio Cartel wealthy, he sent in the Zetas. Hundreds of well-trained soldiers entered Michoacán, outgunning the Valencias, and tipping the balance of power in the state.

In a couple of years, the Valencias were driven out of their home state, fleeing north to join with the Sinaloa Cartel and beginning the journey that would lead to the creation of the CJNG.

But the Zetas truly began to find their fearsome reputation when Heriberto Lazcano, "Z-3," took over in 2004. By then, Guzmán Decena had been shot dead by Mexican security forces, and Cárdenas Guillén was behind bars.

Lazcano was far more ambitious and did not have a particular loyalty to the Gulf Cartel. In a few years, he had recruited many more former soldiers and built military-style training camps across Tamaulipas and other states.[4]

He then sought to grow the Zetas' own power base. While drug trafficking remained a key earner, the Zetas also took over entire towns and made money any way they could: local drug sales, extortion and kidnapping, protection rackets, oil theft and more.

This model allowed them to expand southwards, especially in the states of Coahuila, Nuevo León, and Veracruz. They even reached as far as Guatemala.[5]

WARNING: *The following section of the book contains descriptions of violence that may be upsetting.*

The alliance with the Gulf Cartel finally shattered in 2010, sparking a war which left thousands dead. The Zetas dealt with their enemies implacably. Killing innocent bystanders was not a hindrance. While descriptions of Mexico's cartel wars are always harrowing, the sheer scale of the Zetas' brutality almost beggars belief.

While this book intentionally stays away from sharing graphic descriptions of violence, a brief list is necessary here to explain the depth of hatred and terror the Zetas provoked among the population and their rivals.

In August 2010, the group stopped and kidnapped a group of 75 migrants who were heading to the US border. Reports have diverged over whether the Zetas believed this group worked for the Gulf Cartel, kidnapped them to get ransom from their families, or tried to recruit them. The migrants refused to cooperate, were driven to a farmstead in the municipality of San Fernando, Tamaulipas, and massacred. Only three survived.

In early 2011, the US DEA gave Mexican police contacts crucial information that could lead to the arrests of Zetas leaders Miguel and Omar Treviño, known as "Z-40" and "Z-42." Corrupt policemen passed this information on to the brothers, who quickly came to suspect two of their associates.

Around 60 Zetas gunmen surrounded the community of Allende in Nuevo León connected to the families of the suspected traitors. According to official documents, 42 people were abducted and killed. But, according to witness statements, up to 300 people were massacred.[6] The Allende massacre is the subject of an outstanding Netflix documentary series, "Somos," which respectfully focuses on telling the story from the perspective of those who suffered that day.

In April 2011, in the same town of San Fernando, 193 bodies of Central American migrants were found in mass graves, having been tortured and executed.

In August 2011, the Zetas targeted the Casino Royale in Monterrey whose owner had refused to pay extortion fees. Zetas gunmen burst in, some opened fire, while others poured gasoline around entrances to the building and lit a fire. Fifty-two people died.

And in May 2012, the dismembered torsos of 49 people were left on the side of a road in Cadereyta, Nuevo León.

Many of the horrors that have become common in the Mexican underworld, especially attached to the CJNG, were normalised by the Zetas.

The Zetas' reign of terror would last a few short years. After the arrest of the Treviño brothers in 2013 and 2015, the group lacked an organised leadership, and it succumbed to the cycle of fragmentation that has broken apart many of Mexico's gangs. As of 2023, splinter groups claiming their origins from the Zetas have popped up all over Mexico. Some have become genuine criminal heavyweights of their own, such as the Cartel del Noreste (Northeast Cartel), others control extensive territory in northern and eastern Mexico, such as the Zetas Vieja Escuela (Old School Zetas).

But the impact of the original Zetas is difficult to match.

The Zeta Killers

All this violence could not happen in a vacuum.

On June 18, 2009, as the Zetas were about to break free from the Gulf Cartel, the bodies of three men were found in a gray Jeep Liberty in Cancún. Their hands were tied, and their faces were covered in plastic bags fastened with industrial tape.

Alongside them, a message: "We are the new group 'Matazetas' and we are against kidnapping and extortion, and we will fight against them in all the states for a cleaner Mexico."

Footage would later emerge online of the three men, bound and surrounded by gunmen, confessing to their activities and revealing the names of policemen and politicians who had allegedly been corrupted by the Zetas.[7]

This was but the beginning of a small-scale but persistent campaign targeting the Zetas. Weeks later, in July 2009, four bodies were found next to the road in La Huacana, Michoacán. This time, the message said "We are the Matazetas rebellion. You're next, Rufo."

This threat was aimed at Valdemar Alvarado Benítez, alias "El Rufo," a high-ranking Zetas lieutenant.[8]

Their vendetta against El Rufo began to define the Matazetas. In March 2010, four decapitated heads were left in the town of Apatzingán, in Michoacán, with another message against El Rufo. This time, it was not signed by the Matazetas but by La Resistencia, the name given to a different splinter faction of the Milenio Cartel.

In November 2010, another video emerged of an alleged Zeta member being interrogated and confessing to working for El Rufo before being shot dead.

In 2011, the campaign against the Zetas grew significantly more vicious. On September 20, the bodies of 35 alleged Zeta members were left beneath an underpass in the eastern city of Veracruz, with a video where the Matazetas took credit for the massacre published days later.

Weeks later, on October 6, 32 more people were found dead in two houses near Veracruz. Authorities quickly pinned these killings on the Matazetas as well.

Altogether, around 80 deaths were connected to the Matazetas. However, assigning specific blame for these killings is not easy.

A still from one of the Matazetas videos.

Journalists and commentators continuously describe the CJNG as having once been known as the Matazetas, but the truth is not so clear.

The Matazetas' killings occurred at a time of significant upheaval in the Mexican criminal landscape.

From 2009 to 2011, the Milenio Cartel, as explored earlier in this book, underwent a complete change in leadership. For much of this period, it was under the supervision of Ignacio Coronel, El Chapo's father-in-law and the Sinaloa Cartel boss in Guadalajara.

But the two brothers who led the Milenio Cartel, Óscar Orlando and Juan Nava Valencia, were arrested in 2009 and 2010. Then, Coronel himself was shot dead in July 2010.

The removal of these three crucial leaders left a vacuum at the top, which Mencho rushed to fill. But his ascent was contested by a splinter group of Milenio lieutenants, known as La Resistencia, leading to a brief and brutal civil war.

The Matazetas' killings took place against this complex backdrop, and it seems likely that different factions within the Milenio Cartel used the name. As a further complication, a separate unit within the Sinaloa Cartel, known as Gente Nueva, was also going after the Zetas.[9]

Both the CJNG and the Gente Nueva appear to have used the name Matazetas, likely because this initiative began as a joint effort by the Sinaloa Cartel and Mencho's men.

After 2011, the relationship between the Sinaloa Cartel and the CJNG frayed rapidly, as the newcomers grew quickly and began to rival the Sinaloa Cartel's spread across Mexico.

The Matazetas' campaign ultimately did not have much success. The Zetas' fire would eventually burn itself out as their founding leaders were killed or captured.

So, of all the numerous cartel feuds in Mexico, why has the "Matazetas" name become so legendary? It is frequently incorrectly reported as having been the original name of the CJNG, when at most, the Matazetas were a small portion of the CJNG's membership at the time.

One credible theory is that the Matazetas saga was the first flourish of the public relations campaigns that would help make the CJNG infamous.

The Zetas were at their terrifying peak at the time, boogeymen who made headlines around the world as they represented the worst indulgences of Mexico's cartel violence. The Matazetas stood up to them in a very public way. They struck a chord with their claims of being different, of wanting to defend the people.

The speculation about their identity also helped spread their legend. Were they part of the Sinaloa Cartel? Were they really vigilantes taking the fight to the bad guys?

The signs were there all along that the Matazetas were no Robin Hood figures. It wasn't enough to kill Zeta members, they were butchered and put on display. It wasn't enough to claim responsibility, videos featuring bound and beaten prisoners were published online.

The Matazetas used similar tactics to the Zetas they fought against. And the CJNG has become the successor of the Zetas, at least in the level of public brutality and ruthlessness it has brought to the country.

THE CULT OF MENCHO

Names to Remember:

Nemesio Oseguera Cervantes, alias "Mencho," 57, talismanic leader of the CJNG, one of the men behind the rise in barbaric acts of violence in Mexico, may be dead.

Joaquín Guzmán Loera, alias "El Chapo," 66, founder of the Sinaloa Cartel, jailed for life in the United States.

Rosalinda González Valencia, 61, Mencho's wife, member of the Valencia criminal family, in prison and in ill-health.

Ignacio Coronel, alias "Nacho," high-ranking member of the Sinaloa Cartel and one of Mencho's criminal mentors.

Abraham Oseguera Cervantes, Mencho's brother, who accompanied him to the United States as a young man.

Very few cartel leaders are world-famous.

Pablo Escobar and El Chapo may have their faces plastered on posters, T-shirts and Netflix series. But the real danger in Mexico comes from an aging, moustachioed man who rarely pops his head out of his bolt-hole in the western state of Jalisco.

Mencho has no Netflix shows. Mencho has no clothing line. Almost the only photos of him are prison mugshots taken decades ago.

Escobar and El Chapo cultivated reputations as men of the people, Robin Hood figures who gave generously back to their communities.

Not the case with Mencho. Instead, he has cultivated an aura of fear, devotion and anonymity.

Early Years

Mencho was born in 1966 as Nemesio Rubén Oseguera Cervantes in Naranjo de Chila, an avocado-growing village in the southern state of Michoacán. One of six brothers, he dropped out of school to find work at the age of eleven. At least two of his brothers, Antonio and Abraham, would accompany him into a life of crime.[1]

In that part of Michoacán, there was a natural place to work. The influential Valencia family clan always needed pickers, packers and guards for their extensive avocado plantations around the town of Aguililla.

But young Nemesio soon became involved in the other side of the family business. Under the name of the Milenio Cartel, the Valencias enjoyed a booming marijuana and heroin business, which they sold to Mexico's larger criminal groups.

Some Mexican media reports state that the Valencias spotted Mencho's potential early, and that by the age of 12, he was running a marijuana plantation. While this is a convenient origin story for one of Mexico's most ruthless kingpins, plenty of drug traffickers have embellished their past, and there is no means to confirm exactly how Mencho got his start in the drug trade. He was, however, trusted enough to marry Rosalinda, the oldest daughter of the Valencia family, who quickly became a skilled money launderer like her brothers.[2]

His life path became clearer in his twenties when he ran afoul of American authorities. Like many ambitious, bright-eyed youngsters, Mencho appeared to have become fed up with the country life and moved to California.

America the Beautiful

By 1986, aged 20, he had settled in the San Francisco Bay area. But where many found music, art, or sexual liberation in that gem of a city, Mencho found meth. Police records show Mencho was arrested in 1986 for possession of firearms and stolen property. Officers also suspected he was dealing meth.[3]

This arrest did not put him off. Mencho understood America could give him the skills he needed.

From 1986 to 1994, under a variety of aliases, he zipped back and forth across the border. He was learning skills that laid the foundation for the criminal empire he would come to control: a mastery of how to manufacture, distribute and sell synthetic drugs. He would also lay down roots there. His wife, Rosalinda, would follow him, and their eldest daughter, Jessica Johanna, was born in San Francisco in 1986.[4]

California was the right place to learn. In the late 1980s, the California Valley was the beating heart of the US meth industry. In San Diego, Sacramento and Fresno, huge meth labs would pump out the drug and distribute it to the rest of the United States. Front companies imported the chemicals needed to manufacture meth, mostly from China, and dispatched them to meth labs. This operating model closely resembled the one Mencho would create with the CJNG in Mexico over thirty years later.[5]

Mencho's mugshot after being arrested in San Francisco in May 1986.

There is one example of how he was learning to sniff out trouble, a skill that would serve him later. Court documents tell of how Mencho and his brother, Abraham, found themselves at the Imperial Bar in San Francisco on one evening in 1992. Their goal: to sell five ounces of heroin for $9,500 to two buyers.[6]

According to one wiretapped conversation, Mencho became suspicious about the stacks of crisp-looking hundred-dollar bills the buyers were using. He tipped off Abraham that they were likely undercover policemen.

He was right. It was too late. Authorities had been onto the Cervantes boys for a while, and they were arrested. Mencho served four years in a federal prison in Texas before being turfed back to Mexico in 1997 at the age of 30.[7]

Rise to the Top

Mencho then made an odd lifestyle choice: becoming a police officer. He served for a few years in the towns of Tomátlan and Cabo Corrientes, Jalisco. Very little is known about his time in the police force. But it is difficult to believe he suddenly had an urge to uphold the law.[8]

Tomátlan is a small town south of the major tourist centre of Puerto Vallarta. In the 2010s, it would become a main base for the CJNG where the gang bought property to launder drug money. Perhaps Mencho first laid down roots there when he was a police officer.

His short time in the police force may have also helped him understand its inner workings, how poorly paid and trained Mexican police were, and how open they could be to bribery.

By the early 2000s, he was back in the arms of the Valencia family and their Milenio cartel in Michoacán. As a trusted hand, he was chosen to work as a gunman and bodyguard for the cartel's leader, Armando Cornelio Valencia, alias "Maradona." This lasted until the Valencias made some powerful enemies.[9]

In 2003, the country's most brutal criminal group, the Zetas, commanded by former special forces operatives, invaded Michoacán *(see the chapter on the CJNG's Origins)*. Amid the bloodshed, the Valencia clan was driven out of Michoacán and Maradona was arrested in 2003.[10]

Mencho survived the war with the Zetas and was part of a migration movement north, during which the Valencias sought shelter with El Chapo's Sinaloa Cartel. There was a measure of trust there, since the Valencias were trusted suppliers of marijuana and heroin.

Mencho was put to work under one of the most powerful and ruthless men in the Sinaloa Cartel, Ignacio Coronel, alias "Nacho."

Coronel was the right person to develop Mencho's career. He controlled drug trafficking in and around the city of Guadalajara, one of Mexico's largest, and imported multi-ton shipments of cocaine to send to the United States.

Mencho was handpicked by Coronel to be part of a squad of gunmen who assassinated the Sinaloa Cartel's enemies. Police and press reports from the mid and late 2000s list the Milenio Cartel as operating across much of central and southern Mexico in the name of the Sinaloa Cartel.[11]

Ignacio Coronel Villarreal, alias "Nacho" and and the uncle of El Chapo's wife

This was the perfect stepping block. Mencho developed his leadership skills, gained loyal followers, and furthered his knowledge of Mexico's criminal landscape.

But, within a few years, Mencho's life would be upended again. In 2009 and 2010, several Valencia family leaders were arrested and Coronel was killed in his compound during a raid by the Mexican army. The Milenio Cartel had lost their protector, and they could no longer keep their people united.[12]

Around this time, Mencho gained a troubling reputation: for being a bit of a snitch. As laid out in this book's first chapter, several arrests of his rivals worked out very conveniently for him. Several Milenio Cartel lieutenants believed Mencho may have informed or cooperated with authorities to have them arrested.[13]

This led to a civil war. From 2010 to 2012, an offshoot of the Milenio Cartel refused to acknowledge Mencho and fought each other for control of criminal economies, especially in Jalisco and Michoacán. In a blur of speedily struck and rapidly abandoned criminal alliances, this conflict would also involve other Mexican criminal groups, especially the Zetas.[14]

Eventually, Mencho stood tall. His band of loyal followers, first known as Los Torcidos (The Twisted Ones), formalized into the group known today as the Jalisco Cartel New Generation (CJNG).

Becoming Mexico's Most Wanted

After emerging victorious from the chaos that followed Colonel's death, Mencho began his ascent to Mexico's most-wanted criminal. Almost immediately, he began running the CJNG with open ambition.

While Mencho and the Valencias had come from Michoacán, the CJNG established its base in Jalisco, taking over some of the criminal economies left behind by Coronel.

The fledgling group was tolerated by El Chapo's Sinaloa Cartel at first, as they helped keep common enemies, like the Zetas, at bay.[15]

Mencho embraced traditional forms of criminal income, such as growing and selling marijuana and the opium poppy used to make heroin, as well as trafficking cocaine from South America to the United States.

But increasingly, he steered the group towards the trade he had learned in America: meth.

This pivot provided lavish profits for Mencho and made the CJNG a desirable gang to work for. The resulting influx of numerous gang members in turn allowed Mencho to take his group almost nationwide.

The CJNG's expansion plans followed a well-tested model. Banners would be put up in public areas, announcing the group's arrival into a new city or state. Any who resisted would face a blitzkrieg invasion of CJNG gunmen. Those who were captured often had their bodies displayed as gory warnings.[16 17]

And while Mencho shied away from the limelight personally, the CJNG developed a particular form of gallows humour. In October 2013, three decapitated bodies belonging to a rival outfit, the Knights Templar, were found on a road near Morelia, Michoacán, with a small sign that read: "We are here now… Respectfully, CJNG."[18]

The Pushback

This rapid rise to power made the CJNG a primary target for retaliation by Mexico and the US alike. From 2014 to 2015, Mencho suffered a series of setbacks.

His son, Rubén Oseguera González, alias "Menchito," was arrested in 2014 and again in 2015. Prosecutors depicted Menchito, just 25 at the time, as being a crucial lieutenant to his father who coordinated cocaine deals from South America to Mexico, and gasoline theft in Jalisco, as well as commanding a squad of gunmen to fight against the Zetas and Knights Templar. He was eventually extradited to the US in 2020, where his trial is set to begin in 2024.[19]

The US Office of Foreign Assets Control was also going after the CJNG's money.[20] Mencho was added to the US list of sanctioned individuals in 2015, top CJNG personnel were killed and arrested, and many CJNG-owned properties and businesses were seized.

If the intention was to scare Mencho, or cow him into submission, it didn't work.

Instead, Mencho declared war. In March 2015, a dozen vehicles surrounded police vehicles in Ocotlán, Jalisco, and opened fire. Five police officers were killed and eleven injured. This was just the start.[21]

On April 6, 2015, CJNG gunmen waited for a Mexican police convoy as it wound its way through a mountain highway in northern Jalisco. The vehicles were ambushed as they passed a curve in the road with rock walls on both sides. Gunfire from semi-automatic weapons peppered the vehicles and cut down any officers who tried to get out. Those who sheltered inside were burned alive by grenades and homemade explosives. Fifteen policemen were dead in what became known as the San Sebastián del Oeste ambush.[22]

This remains one of the deadliest single attacks on Mexican security forces by a criminal group.

Then, on May 1, army helicopters spotted a CJNG convoy in which Mencho was believed to be travelling near the town of Villa Purificación in Jalisco. One helicopter, with 18 men on board, was trying to get closer to the convoy when it was hit by two rockets fired from a shoulder-mounted rocket launcher. Several men died at once, according to witness testimony, but others survived even after the helicopter caught fire and crashed to the ground. The gunmen moved in to finish the job and killed several of the survivors before fleeing. Nine Mexican soldiers and policemen lay dead.[23]

Having a military aircraft shot down by a cartel was unheard of in Mexico and this event only enhanced the reputation and coverage of the CJNG as a ruthless threat to national security.

Within days, Jalisco's security chief survived an assassination attempt in which CJNG gunmen pumped 200 bullets and two grenades into his armoured truck.[24]

The message was clear: don't come after Mencho. Ever.

Mexican authorities did back off, but due to unforeseen circumstances. In July 2015, weeks after the frenzied attacks in Jalisco, Mexico's most famous drug kingpin, El Chapo, escaped from a maximum-security prison. The humiliated Mexican government shifted its attention to recapturing him, and the heat on Mencho died down.[25]

2016 would see Mencho confirmed as Mexico's most powerful drug lord, especially after El Chapo was recaptured in January.

His successful defiance of authority, his brazen attacks on Mexican police and his successful wars against criminal rivals across Mexico earned him godlike loyalty among his men. He had also cemented a broad network of police officers, prosecutors, judges and customs officials, which allowed the CJNG's drugs to flow mostly uninterrupted.

An example of this influence came in 2016 when a call between Mencho and a Jalisco police commander was publicly leaked. A furious Mencho can be heard berating the police officer and ordering him to move his men away from a certain area. The commander repeatedly pleads that he will comply and order his troops away, as Mencho insults and threatens him.[26]

Mencho: *Look, you son of a bitch, this is Mencho, man.*

Police Officer: *What?*

Mencho: *Get your fucking people to relax. This is Mencho. Get your fucking men to back off or I am going to kill you and your mother and your whole pack of dogs. I have 30 of you identified. I'm even going to kill your damn dogs if you don't back off. How do you see it?*

Police Officer: *You've got it, Sir. I'll stand them down at once.*

Mencho: *No, no, no. Don't hang up, you son of a bitch. I know where you are.*

This unsettling call, which lasted several minutes, was the final time Mencho's voice is known to have been heard. The voice of a man, heard from off-camera in several CJNG videos published since, has also been claimed to be that of Mencho by Mexican observers.[27]

Mencho Disappears

Mencho's rise to power marked a transition in Mexico's criminal landscape. The brutal Zetas, who terrified Mexico with military-style tactics and lurid brutality, were dismantled. Other pretenders, such as the Gulf Cartel in the northeast of the country, or the Knights Templar in Michoacán, did not have the national presence that the CJNG enjoyed.

The Sinaloa Cartel and the CJNG were the "only two powerful cartels left."[28]

This made them natural enemies, and the war between the Sinaloa Cartel and the CJNG has left thousands dead and continues to rage to this day.

But this level of fame has made Mencho a constant target. The US has placed a $10 million reward for his capture.[29] The Mexican government has put up another $1.5 million.[30]

His wife, Rosalinda, is in prison in reportedly poor health. His son, Menchito, is facing decades behind bars. His brother, Antonio, a senior CJNG boss, was arrested in December 2022 and faces extradition to the United States. Another brother, Abraham, was arrested in April 2024. Most of the Valencia clan he came up with are in prison or dead.

The elusive kingpin himself, however, has essentially vanished. For a time, atrocities were still directly connected to him. In 2017, a popular YouTuber named Juan Luis Lagunas Rosales released a rap in which he said Mencho could "suck his dick". Shortly after, CJNG gunmen entered a bar and shot Lagunas Rosales fifteen times. He was just 17 years old.[31]

But further news about Mencho's whereabouts has almost completely dried up. One important detail that has become common knowledge is that he suffers from severe kidney disease.

According to Mexican security forces, he mostly keeps to a handful of rural mountain villages in Jalisco. In 2020, reports emerged that he had built a small medical facility to attend to him in El Alcíhuatl, a village 250 km southeast of the Jalisco capital, Guadalajara.[32]

His image and name are used frequently by the CJNG in social media posts or on banners, but almost as a cult figure to be revered, not as an active and dangerous kingpin. On special events like Christmas, Easter or Mother's Day, care packages are sometimes distributed by CJNG in villages under their control. Banners were hung which conveyed good wishes from Mencho and bore his picture.[33]

"Mr. Mencho and the CJNG wish a Happy Day to all the Mothers." A banner with Mencho's face hung up in Jalisco in 2021. Source: @Codigo_NegroMX

Reports by the Mexican press have stated he is extremely cautious about using technology and relays orders only through a few hand-picked lieutenants.[34]

But rumours have abounded of his death. In 2015, he was reportedly killed by police in Guadalajara.[35] In 2018, a helicopter apparently opened fire on his convoy and shot him dead.[36] In 2020, Mexico's president, Andrés Manuel López Obrador, personally denied claims that Mencho had died of ill health.[37] And in December 2023, a song, entitled "Ya Se Fue" (He's Already Gone), was released on YouTube directly claiming Mencho had died.[38]

Some CJNG allies have certainly believed it. In early 2022, Los Mezcales, a small gang in Colima, turned on the CJNG and stated on banners that Mencho was dead. "I only owe respect and loyalty to Mencho," stated the Mezcales' leader.[39]

The response was rapid. Violence erupted and La Vaca was quickly killed. The CJNG-Mezcales feud left dozens dead. But despite all this, the CJNG has provided no concrete evidence Mencho is alive.

This is almost certainly by design. If healthy, Mencho may wish to remain invisible, knowing that to show himself will bring trouble. If sick, he may wish to hide his weakness. If dead, the CJNG may want to avoid fragmentation.

He also serves as a major distraction. As one of the most-wanted men in Mexico and the United States, Mencho is a lightning rod. His face is plastered on most-wanted lists while his family and assets are sanctioned, but this ultimately does little to engage with the more complex reality of the CJNG.

Mexico's most powerful narco has become a boogeyman.

THE RISE AND FALL OF THE CUINIS

The name "Cuinis" is constantly associated with the CJNG. From US sanctions and Mexican police reports, the CJNG and the Cuinis are mentioned side by side.

But who were the Cuinis? Were they the richest cartel in the world, as one DEA source described them?[1]

Were they the CJNG's moneymen? International meth traffickers? A faction within the CJNG, or even its real leaders, as has been suggested?

None of these truly captures the unique symbiotic relation that existed between the CJNG and the Cuinis. More specifically, this symbiosis came from the friendship between CJNG boss, Mencho, and his brother-in-law, Abigael González Valencia, alias "El Cuini."

Abigael was born in Aguililla, Michoacán, in 1972, when Mencho was already six years old. He was one of a colossal brood of siblings, born into an avocado-growing clan. The number of siblings has been variously placed at 15 or 18. Not all of them appear in the records of the CJNG. Either way, the González Valencia family were so numerous they were nicknamed the Cuiniques, or "Cuinis," in reference to a local, highly fertile squirrel.[2]

Early Beginnings

Much like Mencho, Abigael and many of his brothers and sisters got started early in the drug trade. In the '80s, the González Valencia family began working in the Milenio Cartel's marijuana and heroin operations.

The close ties between the family and Mencho soon began to foster. He fell in love with the eldest sister of the Cuinis, Rosalinda González Valencia. She and Abigael would follow Mencho to San Francisco to learn the ins and outs of the flourishing meth trade and to found their own drug distribution network. Rosalinda would even give birth to Mencho's two eldest children in San Francisco, Jessica Johanna in July 1986 and Ruben in February 1990.[3]

The Cuinis' exact role in the glory days of the Milenio Cartel is unclear, but they acquired crucial knowledge that served the CJNG very well twenty years later. While the Valencia family began by selling their own marijuana and heroin, the 1990s saw them expand rapidly.

Abigael and his siblings were front-and-centre as the Milenio Cartel first expanded into cocaine, becoming crucial partners to Pablo Escobar's Medellín Cartel in the mid-1990s, and then into methamphetamine.

While Mencho was arrested in 1994 and served three years in prison in the US before being released in 1997, Abigael avoided arrest until 1996. In May 1996, he was arrested in California and charged with manufacturing, possession and conspiracy to distribute meth in the cities of Fresno and Madera.

Unlike Mencho, Abigael didn't stick around. He posted bail worth $80,000 in November 1996, and was ordered to reappear in court in April 1997, but simply went home.[4]

For the next period of Milenio Cartel history, the Cuinis went quiet. In 1999, Operation Milenio revealed the Valencias' ties to the Medellin Cartel, and their entire organization had to be restructured.

A brief alliance with the Gulf Cartel from 2000 to 2002 to smuggle marijuana, cocaine, heroin and meth through the northeastern state of Tamaulipas collapsed in spectacular fashion. When the Gulf Cartel's enforcers, the Zetas, drove the Milenio Cartel out of Michoacán in 2003, several of the Cuinis fled north.

The Cuinis began working for the Sinaloa Cartel in the state of Jalisco, as did Mencho, but attacks by the Zetas did not cease. This period provides some insight as to when the Cuinis began to ascend to leadership positions.

On August 2, 2005, Zetas gunmen stormed a ranch in Tonalá, Jalisco, where numerous Milenio Cartel members were attending a cockfight. Two grenades were thrown into the crowd before the gunmen opened fire. Four people were killed, and 28 people were injured. Abigael's younger brother, José, was shot in the arm, and Mencho's brother, Antonio, was also hurt.

When investigating the case, Mexican police would briefly arrest two other Cuinis, Edgar and Luis Angel, for trying to sneak their brother out of the hospital.[5]

This marked the first time the González Valencia siblings appeared prominently in Mexican police reports.

Money Laundering Experts

While the Valencias were under the orders of the Sinaloa Cartel in the mid-2000s, the Cuinis were already developing expertise in financial crime and money laundering. The Milenio Cartel continued to coordinate massive shiploads of cocaine arriving through the port of Manzanillo, but this time, the Sinaloa Cartel took the lion's share of the proceeds.

Former Milenio Cartel boss Óscar Nava Valencia revealed to a US court that Abigael González Valencia, the head of the Cuinis had forged ties with a Colombian drug trafficking clan known as the Rastrojos long before the CJNG even existed.

Nava Valencia stated that he had personally invested in three shipments of Colombian cocaine, weighing 1.5 tons each, which Abigael had been in charge of bringing to Mexico between 2006 and 2007.

In November 2007, evidence emerged that the Cuinis were also beginning to launder large sums of money through the tourism industry, first in Jalisco, and then in the rest of Mexico. Another Cuini brother, Gerardo and his wife, Wendy, bought the Hotelito Desconocido at a beautiful tourist spot on the Jalisco coast through an architectural firm serving as a front company.[6]

The Hotelito Desconocido in Jalisco.

But more upheaval soon engulfed the Milenio Cartel. Relationships between the Valencia leadership and their Sinaloa Cartel paymasters grew tense. In 2009 and 2010, the Milenio Cartel underwent a real crisis of leadership as several of its main leaders were arrested one after another *(see chapter on the CJNG's Origins).*

The Valencia family, including the Cuinis, backed Mencho as the new leader, but others disagreed. Mencho's backers became Los Torcidos (The Twisted Ones), while his opponents founded La Resistencia (The Resistance). A bitter series of tit-for-tat murders ensued for a few months in 2010 until Mencho made a crucial power play.

He made a deal with the Sinaloa Cartel, he would become the leader of operations and head of the Milenio Cartel, but defer to the larger group as his overlords. His second-in-command would be his brother-in-law, Abigael.

This new outfit would become the CJNG we know today. And the Cuinis would only grow in power.

With La Resistencia sidelined, the Sinaloa Cartel and the CJNG could turn their attention to more dangerous foes: the Zetas. But while Mencho appears to have been involved in the Matazetas campaign *(see chapter on the Matazetas)*, the Cuinis took a different tactic.

According to numerous media reports and court documents, the Cuinis sought to curry favour from officials and policemen in areas the CJNG controlled to set up a colossal money laundering operation.

Throughout the early 2010s, the siblings expanded front companies in a range of industries, including construction, organic produce, alcoholic beverages and real estate. Two Cuinis, Erika and Ulises, were particularly involved in the scheme. While their money laundering fronts would spread around Mexico, these early iterations were focused in Jalisco, where the Cuinis were accused of bribing high-ranking members of the judiciary and the state government.[7]

Parallel to this, the Cuinis' leader, Abigael, was busy finding alternative ways of doing business. While Mencho was leading the CJNG to become a nationally powerful cartel, Abigael explored different options.

On the money laundering side, the Cuinis expanded outside Jalisco and began buying front businesses in other popular tourist sites, where cash-intensive industries proved useful. A report by the US Office of Foreign Assets Control (OFAC) from 2016 showed the Cuinis and the CJNG owned a shopping centre, holiday homes, an advertising company, and a sushi restaurant.[8]

International Meth Lords

In 2013, Europol warned that "Mexican criminal groups are attempting to establish themselves as key players in the European drugs market," with the Sinaloa Cartel identified by name.[9]

In its 2015 National Drug Threat Assessment, the DEA would then state that the CJNG "rivals the Sinaloa Cartel trafficking operations in Asia, Europe, and Oceania," with the Cuinis providing the expansion for this funding.

The Sinaloa Cartel's expansion model, sourcing precursor chemicals from China, moving meth to East Asia and Australia, and having some involvement in the cocaine trade to Europe and West Africa has been well documented.[10]

There is evidence that the CJNG, driven by the Cuinis' international focus, followed this model. For example, a shipment of 131 kilograms of meth found in Barcelona in November 2014, hidden inside tins of pineapple, is strongly believed to have come from the CJNG, according to investigators. This meth had come from Jalisco and was the highest-ever seizure of the drug ever made in Europe at the time.[11]

But even the European connection of this shipment is contested, since Spanish investigators stated it was bound for Australia.[12]

Similarly, Abigael is known to have visited Spain in the early days of the CJNG, allegedly buying properties, including in Barcelona, to launder money that may have come from local drug deals.[13]

Similarly, while the CJNG was mentioned as early as 2013 as shipping meth to Australia, the extent of this at the time was not clear. The country has a high number of meth users and the complexity of moving drugs there is rewarded by some of the highest sale prices in the world. Mexican cartels have had a lucrative partnership, distributing meth wholesale to Australian biker gangs who would then distribute it.[14]

There is little evidence to suggest that the CJNG avoided the US market. In 2016, a US Treasury Department report described the CJNG as distributing cocaine and meth along "10,000 kilometers of the Pacific coast in a route that extends from the Southern Cone to the border of the United States and Canada."[15]

The Arrests Begin

Impressive as they were, the Cuinis' activities would suffer a crippling blow on February 28, 2015. Abigael was arrested while dining with Colombian and Venezuelan associates at a restaurant in Puerto Vallarta, Jalisco, a town where the Cuinis owned several properties.

While many other Cuinis were involved to varying degrees in criminal operations for the CJNG, Abigael was the uncontested leader. His arrest triggered a series of actions against the CJNG and the González Valencia family.

The US and Mexico alike smelled blood and ramped up their investigations. In June 2015, Mencho's son, Ruben Oseguera González, alias "Menchito," was also detained in Zapopan, Jalisco, after a tip-off. Menchito was not as secretive as his father and was regularly seen in public.

The Hotelito Desconocido, one of the Cuinis' first fronts, was shut down.

In August, Mencho's brother, Antonio, alias "Tony Montana," was also caught in Jalisco.

The Cuinis began falling like dominoes. Abigael's brother, Elvis, a top financial operator for the CJNG, was shot by a rival group as he relieved himself by the roadside in January 2016. He survived but was arrested by authorities in hospital.

The second most influential Cuini, Gerardo, had been on the police's radar after a Panama Papers investigation in 2015 revealed several international transactions connected to him.[16] Gerardo had been busy hiding the cartel's millions in other parts of Latin America. Since 2009, he and his wife had opened substantial businesses in Argentina, including a supermarket chain, a corner store, a storage facility, a bar and café, and other shops that never opened. In Uruguay, he owned a multi-million-dollar property and luxury vehicles.[17]

In April 2016, Gerardo was living in Montevideo, Uruguay, and was arrested by Uruguayan police along with his wife and father-in-law.

In 2017, José González Valencia was arrested, while on holiday with his family in Brazil. He had been living permanently in Bolivia where he owned property and had developed a reputation as a cattle breeder under a false name.

Cuinis' arrests would continue to happen in later years, including Arnulfo and Ulises Jovani, in 2018, but by then, the brothers' power had been largely diminished.[18]

Las Cuinis Take Over

The big sister stepped up. Rosalinda, Mencho's wife and Abigael's sister, had already been a formidable part of the CJNG-Cuinis ensemble. But following Abigael's arrest, she took over his web of money laundering fronts with superlative skill.

From 2018 to 2021, when Rosalinda is believed to have run the CJNG's finances, authorities in Mexico seized almost 900 million pesos ($55 million) in assets across more than 10,000 bank accounts. These were in the names of her relatives, other CJNG members, restaurant owners, businessmen, and even local politicians. She was connected to laundering attempts through numerous types of business, including a car wash.[19]

Known as "La Jefa," Rosalinda was ably surrounded.

A number of her sisters, especially Maria Ivette, Berenice and Noemí, were listed by US authorities as helping the CJNG to launder money and traffic drugs to the United States, although further details have not been provided.[20]

Two of her sisters-in-law, Jennifer Beaney Camacho Cázares, the wife of Abigael, and Wendy Delaithy Amaral Arévalo, the wife of Gerardo, were also prominently involved and listed as owners of multiple businesses connected to the CJNG in Jalisco, the rest of Mexico and abroad.

Finally, Rosalinda's daughter, Jessica Johanna, stepped into the family business. She was listed by OFAC as owner or part-owner of six businesses in Mexico used for money laundering. She was also allegedly in charge of keeping financial accounts of drug debts owed to the CJNG.[21]

As the Cuinis began to fall, Rosalinda knew she would be a prominent target. Between 2015 and 2018, as they became the increasing focus of US investigations, Rosalinda and Jessica Johanna repeatedly filed for writs of *amparo*. This complex Mexican legal tool can help protect a citizen from alleged persecution and arrest. However, these were denied.[22]

On May 26, 2018, Rosalinda was arrested in Zapopan, Jalisco and soon put on trial.

Things did not go smoothly for the prosecution, however. The judge ruled that her direct connections to the CJNG were not proven and dropped a charge of involvement in organised crime. A charge for money laundering did stick, but Rosalinda was released on bail after she agreed to pay 1.5 million Mexican pesos.

While Rosalinda was freed, her trial for money laundering was supposed to continue, but it does not appear this was the case.

Rosalinda would be arrested again in 2021 after failing to check in with police every two weeks as set in the conditions of her 2018 bail. In December 2023, she was sentenced to five years in prison for hiding financial transactions from a car wash she owned. During her trial, it was revealed that she is reportedly suffering from severe kidney issues, requiring immunosuppressive therapy.

As for her children, they would both spend time behind bars.

In February 2020, Jessica Johanna flew to Washington, DC to attend the trial of her younger brother, Rubén, who had just been extradited to the United States to face drug trafficking charges. She was arrested inside the courthouse, with a significant amount of cash on her and wearing a Rolex watch, a Louis Vuitton coat, and a Hermes bag.

The prosecutions of both of Mencho's children have proven complicated. Ruben first pleaded not guilty to trafficking drugs to the US in 2020 and the case was set to go to trial. This caused significant anticipation as Menchito would have been the first senior CJNG leader to have his case go to trial and revelations about the cartel's upper echelons might have emerged.

The amount of evidence meant the trial took several years to come together. But in March 2023, mere weeks before the trial was set to open, Ruben notified prosecutors he now wished to plead guilty. According to legal observers, this was likely because a plea deal had been reached, in which Ruben would plead guilty and avoid trial in exchange for significant cooperation. But in April 2023, the day before his plea was to be entered, Ruben backed out. As of writing, his trial is scheduled to take place in 2024.[23]

Jessica made a tenacious defence for a year before pleading guilty in March 2021, and was sentenced to 30 months in prison for violating the US Kingpin Act and continuing to operate businesses sanctioned by the United States. She was released in early 2022.

With Mencho's wife, son, and numerous brothers-in-law now in prison, the Cuinis have ceased to function as a major criminal threat and their money laundering operations have been rolled out into the CJNG itself.

Where are the Cuinis?

Abigael González Valencia, alias "El Cuini," arrested in 2015, remains in prison in Mexico despite repeated attempts by the US to have him extradited.

Arnulfo González Valencia was sentenced to five years in prison in Mexico in 2019 for trafficking cocaine and meth.

Elvis González Valencia remains in prison after being arrested in Mexico for electoral crimes in 2019.

Gerardo González Valencia, alias "Lalo," arrested in 2016 in Uruguay, was sentenced to life in prison in the United States in July 2023.

José González Valencia, arrested in Brazil in 2017, pled guilty to cocaine trafficking charges in the US in 2022.

Jessica Johanna Oseguera González, alias "La Negra," was released in 2023 after serving over two years in prison for violating the US Kingpin Act.

Rosalinda González Valencia, alias "La Jefa," was sentenced to five years in prison in Mexico for financial irregularities in December 2023.

Ruben Oseguera González, alias "El Menchito," is awaiting trial in the US on drug trafficking charges.

Ulises Jovani González Valencia was sentenced to six years in prison in Mexico in 2019 for trafficking cocaine and meth.

Abigail, Arnulfo, Berenice, Edgar Eden, Maria Elena, Marisa Ivette, and Noemí González Valencia, all sanctioned or identified as CJNG associates by the United States, remain at large.

***information correct as of April 2024.**

THE NEXT GENERATION OF CJNG LEADERS

Mencho might be dying, or already dead. Even if not, he's in his late fifties and seemingly in ill health. His death (or arrest) would present an interesting challenge to the CJNG's longevity as an organized group.

While it has been resilient in the face of fragmentation, Mencho's presence as a unifying figure has been crucial to the group's public face. As discussed in this book, his name and face are used prominently by the CJNG across Mexico. Some groups, such as the Mezcales in Colima, have already broken away from the CJNG claiming Mencho had died.[1]

Yet, for a group as widespread as the CJNG to retain control over local economies, powerful lieutenants have emerged who could seek to contest the throne, once Mencho is gone.

It is uncertain to what extent loyalty to the CJNG's roots in Michoacán will play a part. Mencho was the first non-Valencia to take control of the group, but he was married to a Valencia and had grown up working on the clan's avocado plantations.

In the years since, the CJNG has become a many-headed hydra, with powerful contenders, each with their own followings, and some who have little to no connection to the Valencias. Keeping the CJNG united after the death or removal of Mencho will require a powerful, respected central figure. If such a leader fails to appear, this could trigger a violent cycle of fragmentation as different lieutenants break away.

Here are the profiles of four leading figures within the CJNG who could all fancy their chances.

This information is accurate as of April 2024. However, the arrest or death of any of those listed below could significantly change the composition of the CJNG's future leadership or the cartel's chances of remaining united.

Juan Carlos Valencia González, alias "Pelón" or "R3"

R3 was born to Rosalinda Valencia González when she worked as an undocumented worker in California, prior to her marriage with Mencho.[2]

Mencho became R3's stepfather when he was around two years old and the pair appear to have developed a close bond. R3 is consistently reported to be one of Mencho's closest advisors and in constant touch with the reclusive CJNG leader.

His criminal career predates the formation of the CJNG since US authorities have accused him of trafficking cocaine and meth from Mexico to the US since at least 2007.[3]

The 2015 arrest of Mencho's son, Rubén Oseguera González, alias "Menchito," left room at the top. Since then, R3 has been connected to several prominent CJNG actions.[4]

He is commonly associated with Grupo Elite, one of the CJNG's main armed wings which has intervened in prominent hotspots across Mexico, including Guanajuato and Michoacán.[56] In 2021, the US Department of State issued a $5 million reward for information leading to his arrest.[7]

Despite his fame, R3, like his stepfather Mencho, has kept a low profile. Instead, he may use his close friendship with another CJNG lieutenant on this list, Ricardo Ruiz Velasco, alias "Doble R," to enact his will.[8]

Their friendship is prominently mentioned in a narco-ballad about Doble R, which may also hint at R3's future leadership ambitions. *"In this life, there must be gratitude for Sir Mencho and his son, El Tres (The Three) who is more than my friend. I give them my thanks for being two very fine men, we remain ready to open a gap in their path,*" sings the group Marca Registrada.[9]

Audias Flores-Silva, alias "Jardinero"

Jardinero has been quietly building a criminal fiefdom in Mexico and the US.

Born in 1980, Jardinero is a Michoacán native and hails from Huetamo, a town at the center of repeated battles between drug trafficking gangs. He began his career in the CJNG as chief of security for Mencho, before taking on a progressively larger role.[10]

According to Mexican and American authorities, he is primarily based in the state of Nayarit. From there, he runs CJNG operations in much of western Mexico, including a network of labs manufacturing fentanyl and meth being sent to the US. US authorities have also accused him of trafficking cocaine from Central America to the US through tractor-trailer trucks and passenger vehicles.[11]

He has extensive experience trafficking drugs across the border. He was arrested in 2002 in North Carolina and sentenced to five years in prison for trafficking drugs, before being sent back to Mexico.[12]

In 2015, a police convoy was ambushed by CJNG gunmen near the village of Soyatán in Jalisco. Fifteen officers were killed and five more injured, with Jardinero believed to have been partially responsible for organising the attack. He was arrested in connection to the massacre in 2016, but the charges didn't stick, and he was freed within weeks.[13]

Since then, his status within the CJNG has continued to grow. He is allegedly behind a group of CJNG soldiers who specialise in extorting lime farmers. The US has issued a $5 million reward for information leading to his arrest.[14][15]

In November 2023, he had a narrow escape when police raided his luxury apartment in Zapopan, Jalisco. This raid came days after an ambush in Zacatecas, which left three soldiers dead and was blamed on Jardinero. He had been posing as a businessman and art collector in Zapopan, but he escaped before the police arrived.[16][17]

Jardinero's fame as a CJNG leader and the significant attention he has received in both Mexico and the US makes it likely that efforts to track and capture him will continue.

Ricardo Ruiz Velasco, alias "Doble R", "RR" or "R2"

RR may be approaching the upcoming succession battle within the CJNG in the same way a politician might. On Christmas Eve 2022, a convoy of trucks decorated with Christmas baubles made its way through the neighbourhood of El Retiro in Guadalajara, Jalisco.

Laden with TV screens, home appliances and toys, the trucks were obviously from the CJNG. Videos of the event circulated online with the title "Mr. RR is distributing presents." People receiving the presents were also encouraged to thank Mencho for the cameras.[18]

The message was inescapable: Mencho and RR were being lauded at the same time.

RR has certainly worked hard to ascend the ranks, being involved in many significant CJNG battlefronts. He was arrested at least 15 times between 2002 and 2009, for drug trafficking, theft and assault, among other petty crimes.[19]

But since joining the ranks, RR has played crucial roles in the group. In 2015, he was reportedly in Aguascalientes in charge of large-scale drug trafficking to the US. From 2017, he was one of the leaders of Grupo Elite, one of the CJNG's original strike forces, who regularly show off their armoured cars and heavy weaponry. Under his command, Grupo Elite has been deployed in Guanajuato to fight the Santa Rosa de Lima Cartel in 2020 and then in Michoacán to reclaim the CJNG's birthplace of Aguililla.[20]

According to the latest police reports, he is believed to head up CJNG operations in Michoacán, Guanajuato, Zacatecas and Aguascalientes, all crucial pieces of criminal real estate.[21]

The loyalty he inspires became clear in August 2022. After police reports indicated RR had been arrested, CJNG gunmen turned out in force in Jalisco and Guanajuato. Gang members opened fire on security forces, cars were burned and blockades were set up on main thoroughfares. After three days of chaos, President Andrés Manuel López Obrador was forced to admit that RR had never been captured after all.[22]

However, RR's close friendship with Mencho's stepson, Juan Carlos, raises questions about whether he would be chosen above a Valencia.

Gonzalo Mendoza Gaytán, alias "El Sapo"

El Sapo *(The Frog)* is the CJNG's man in Puerto Vallarta, one of the most important hubs for the Mexican cartel. From there, he controls a colossal money laundering and drug trafficking network that stretches across Mexico to the Caribbean coasts of Veracruz and Tabasco.[23] His wife, Liliana Rosas Camba, is accused of also being a prominent money launderer and both have been sanctioned by the US.[24]

Gonzalo Mendoza Gaytán and Liliana Rosas Camba

He was named as second-in-command to Mencho in a Ministry of Defense document about criminal networks in western Mexico that was made public during a leak of government papers. While designing him in that specific role is up for debate, there is no doubt he holds considerable power within the cartel.[25]

El Sapo is a major target for the Mexican government as he has been connected to high-profile assassinations as well as rampant extortion and kidnappings. Authorities have also stated El Sapo was likely behind the 2020 assassination of former Jalisco governor Aristóteles Sandoval, one of the most high-profile political hits ever carried out by the CJNG.[26]

El Sapo has also headed up CJNG operations in Los Altos, a northeastern region of Jalisco on the border with Sinaloa. A CJNG armed wing based there, the Grupo Élite Delictivo de Reacción Inmediata (GEDDRI), have been battling the Sinaloa and the Nueva Plaza cartels.[27]

And in line with many drug bosses before him, El Sapo may have a passion for tigers, being connected to a zoo in Puerto Vallarta which allegedly breeds the big cats for cartel members.[28]

THE CJNG's MONEY LAUNDERING EMPIRE

From its earliest days, the CJNG was making sound financial decisions. It invested wisely, pumping money into a range of industries in Mexico and around the world.

A crucial aspect to this plan was the separation of the CJNG's efforts into two distinct entities. Mencho and the CJNG proper could focus on expanding a physical criminal empire across Mexico, while the Cuinis, led by Mencho's brother-in-law, concentrated on the financial side (*see The Rise and Fall of the Cuinis chapter*).

In a few short years, the CJNG had a money laundering empire that stretched from hotels on Mexico's Pacific Coast to the tourist district of Barcelona and luxury properties in Uruguay.[1]

Even after the Cuinis were progressively dismantled in the 2010s, other opportunities presented themselves. Trade-based money laundering has allowed the CJNG to move huge drug profits from the United States to Mexico. The Chinese underground banking system has also become a boon for Mexican cartels, including the CJNG, through which they launder tens of millions of dollars undetected.[2]

And with cryptocurrency, the CJNG has gained access to various financial scams and phishing schemes.

Here, we break down the major types of financial crimes carried out by the Mexican cartel.

Front Businesses in Mexico

The CJNG likes to invest locally. Its base in Mexico's western state of Jalisco, as well as other states along the Pacific Coast, is home to the lion's share of its money laundering schemes through brick-and-mortar businesses.

The influence of the Cuinis, an extensive clan of siblings from the Valencia family, was evident before the CJNG was even independent. In November 2007, Gerardo González Valencia and his wife bought a hotel, the Hotelito Desconocido, on the Jalisco coast.[3]

The hotel became infamous because several fishermen who were in a dispute with the new owners disappeared in 2011.[4] It also served as an example of how well-informed the Cuinis and the CJNG were about potential backlashes. In August 2015, the hotel was seized by authorities after being designated as connected to the CJNG by the US under its Foreign Narcotics Kingpin Designation Act.[5]

But three months prior, Gerardo had quietly sold the hotel to another company, which had to bear the cost of its shutdown.

Since the late 2000s, the CJNG has bought colossal amounts of real estate and companies in numerous sectors in Jalisco. In 2015, the US Treasury Department took its first real action against the Cuinis. In addition to the Jalisco hotel, US authorities listed two real estate firms and a shopping centre in Jalisco, as well as another mall across the country in Playa del Carmen, as belonging to the CJNG's money laundering network.[6]

Progressive US and Mexican investigations would gradually reveal more and more connections within this money laundering network. Despite an increasing international portfolio, the CJNG's business interests remained firmly rooted in Jalisco.

Between 2015 and 2020, at least 90 businesses were seized in Mexico after being suspected of being owned by the CJNG and the Cuinis. Eighty-two percent of these were in Jalisco, with the rest scattered around Mexico City, the State of Mexico, Quintana Roo and Colima.[7]

Trade-Based Money Laundering

In 2020, the threat of the CJNG to the United States had grown so severe that the DEA and the Department of Justice launched Project Python, a multi-agency operation seeking to tackle the cartel's drug trafficking and financial networks at the same time.

In six months, Project Python seized over $20 million suspected of belonging to the CJNG. It also revealed ample details about the way the group moved the money collected from selling fentanyl, meth, heroin and more in the US back to Mexico. The DEA estimated the CJNG was collecting a minimum of $8 billion a year, with the real number likely far higher.[8]

Given the quantities involved, the CJNG has become increasingly involved in trade-based money laundering. This process involves laundering illicit funds by using them in what appear to be legitimate cross-border commercial transactions between companies and international money brokers. The specifics of the import and export trades, such as their price, value, quantity, and quality, can then be manipulated to help mask the funds.[9]

The CJNG also heavily favours the black market peso exchange, a type of trade-based money laundering that manipulates currency exchange to transfer drug money back to Mexico.

The CJNG sells dollars from drug sales to middlemen who then find Mexican businesses eager to buy American goods. These businesses pay in pesos, which the middlemen use to pay the cartels, while the dollars buy the goods from the US, making every transaction look legitimate.[10]

Many of the businesses unwittingly involved as the individual transactions they are involved in appear legitimate, according to the DEA.[11]

Since Project Python, trade-based money laundering networks have continued to be uncovered. In 2023, Mary Cruz Rodríguez Aguirre, a one-time political candidate and businesswoman, was accused by the US of running such a network for Audias Flores-Silva, alias "El Jardinero" (The Gardener), a leading CJNG commander. Rodríguez Aguirre owned a currency exchange house and a network of US businesses to allegedly launder over $6 million.[12]

Early International Money Laundering Attempts

Even before the CJNG was its own entity, the Cuinis sought to launder significant profits in Latin America and Europe, showcasing their innovation.

Gerardo González Valencia, brother-in-law to Mencho, and his wife, Wendy Dalaithy Amaral Arévalo, appeared to have been the prime movers behind this strategy. From 2007 to 2011, the couple lived in Argentina. With the help of an Argentine businessman, Oscar Gilberte Vaz de Sousa, they opened a convenience store in Buenos Aires through which they are believed to have laundered $1.8 million.[13]

In 2012, Gerardo and Wendy moved to Uruguay, settling in the tourist city of Punta del Este. The Panama Papers investigation would reveal that the Cuinis had created two companies, Montella Global SA and Deltodo Enterprises, through Mossack Fonseca, the Panamanian law firm at the center of the scandal.[14] They also bought real estate in Uruguay, as well as luxury cars, which had been placed in the names of their domestic employees. The two firms were also connected to industrial properties in China and Russia.

They were arrested in Uruguay in 2016, and Gerardo was later extradited to the US and sentenced to life in prison.[15]

Another Cuini brother, José González Valencia, chose Bolivia as his new base.[16]

Prior to this, he was reportedly in charge of providing security to Mencho, and for running an arms trafficking operation between Central America, Mexico and the United States. In 2016, he entered Bolivia under a fake identity and bought a residence in the city of Santa Cruz de la Sierra. From there, he entered the cattle business, breeding Zebu cows and even winning prizes at fairs for the quality of his livestock. In December 2017, he was arrested while holidaying in Brazil and eventually extradited to the US.[17]

The head of the Cuinis, Abigael Gonzalez Valencia, is also known to have travelled to Europe and bought properties in Barcelona's tourist area of Las Ramblas.[18]

The Chinese Shadow Banking System

China's labyrinthine chemicals industry has made it relatively easy for Mexican drug traffickers to find sellers for fentanyl and chemical precursors to manufacture synthetic drugs for decades. Consequently, China's equally opaque banking system has also been used to smuggle transfers and proceeds from a wide range of Latin American criminal organisations, including Mexico's leading cartels.[19]

But a number of arrests and raids in the last decade have shown just how deeply cartels, such as the CJNG and the Sinaloa Cartel, rely on their Chinese counterparts to move, hide and launder illicit funds.[20]

The most noteworthy such operation was run by an admittedly brilliant money laundering expert named Li Xizhi. A Chinese national who moved to California as a teenager, Li soon became associated with the 14K, one of the largest Chinese organised crime groups, commonly known as the Triads.[21]

He rapidly became involved in Mexico-China criminal connections, especially drug trafficking and migrant smuggling. However, he soon developed a complex money laundering scheme between Mexican drug cartels and rich Chinese citizens looking to get their money out of China. Cartel members in the US would give hundreds of thousands in dollars to couriers working for Li. Li would then order the transfer of the equivalent amount in Mexican pesos to designated cartel contacts in Mexico.[22]

The US dollars were then provided to members of the Chinese diaspora in New York or Los Angeles, either in cash, bank deposits, cashier's checks, or as chips at casinos. Finally, the clients in China would transfer the same amount in yuan to accounts Li controlled in China. Li would take a 1-2% commission from such transactions, which was far lower than what brokers in other similar money laundering schemes took.[23]

Li was eventually arrested in Mexico in 2019 and extradited to the US, where he received a 15-year sentence. He is alleged to have laundered hundreds of millions of dollars. While he mostly worked for the Sinaloa Cartel, the scale of the scams he ran has led to widespread suspicions he also collaborated with the CJNG.

Cryptocurrencies

The CJNG is believed to have laundered billions in drug money through Bitcoin and other cryptocurrencies by using them to sidestep scrutiny from banks and national authorities.

In its 2016 National Drug Threat Assessment, the DEA noted that Bitcoin was used by Mexican criminal organizations to pay companies in China that were providing counterfeit goods and chemical precursors.[24]

By 2020, it had become clear how the CJNG was playing a leading role in standardizing the use of Bitcoin to hide suspicious transactions. That year, Mexico noted 1,033 transfers involving Bitcoin that exceeded the legal threshold of 56,000 pesos per transaction. Above this threshold, cryptocurrency exchanges must register these transactions with authorities. Over 98% of these excessive transfers came from the state of Jalisco, with Mexican financial watchdogs heavily suspecting they were linked to the CJNG.[25]

Registering these transactions is useful to localise the source of transactions but has not led to much direct action. Mexican cartels like the CJNG also employ "tumblers," cryptocurrency experts who can mix identifiable crypto transfers with illegal funds, making them harder to distinguish.

In 2022, the Russian dark web marketplace Hydra was taken down by American and German law enforcement. Following this raid, a number of accounts connected to the CJNG and the Sinaloa Cartel were found, indicating that the cartels may have engaged in cryptocurrency-backed selling of drugs via the platform.[26]

A patchwork of insufficient laws and regulatory frameworks across Latin America mean that cryptocurrency scams and money laundering perpetrated by Mexican cartels will only continue to grow, according to Global Financial Integrity.[27]

THE CJNG'S GIFT FOR PUBLIC RELATIONS

The little hits of dopamine from TikTok views are just as seductive for cartel gunmen as for social media addicts. The CJNG has developed its own social media branding, which follows in the footsteps of plenty of other cartels before it, especially the Zetas.

For example, a little purple devil emoji (😈) is featured in posts by the CJNG or its fans on social media, whether playing Grand Theft Auto V or dismembering a rival.

But what do such groups get out of using social media? Well, displays of violence or lavish shows of wealth published by cartels have well-documented real-life impacts.

Vulnerable young people can be lured in by promises of a glamorous lifestyle. Respect or belief in security institutions (admittedly thin on the ground in Mexico) can be eroded by viewing cartel members behave as they wish, in public, with no consequences. The power these groups wield over communities is increased when they show themselves providing key services.

Mexican cartels are masters of propaganda, and in far more subtle ways than commonly believed. Going back 15 years, cartel presence on social media has reflected the same values that they seem to represent on the streets, according to a report by the Global Network on Extremism & Technology (GNET).[1]

The promotion of the criminal way of life, the reinforcement of hyper-masculine narratives about wealth, power and sex, and the development of cults of personality are present in numerous social media interactions one can have with organised crime in Mexico.

And rival criminal groups engage in the same cycle of one-upmanship on social media as regular people. But instead of selfies and holiday snaps, this is played out through increasingly lurid displays of violence and wealth.

Below, the World of Crime uses the categories of such social media use, put forward by GNET:

- **The promotion of *narcocultura***: Guns, cars, drugs, money, clothes, jewelry and houses are all shown off in lavish displays, which helps to appeal to some young people struggling economically. The most successful recent example of this is the #Chapiza hashtag deployed by the Chapitos, the sons of Sinaloa leader, Joaquín Archivaldo Guzmán Loera, alias "El Chapo."

- **Machismo**: The gang lifestyle is fetishised as an ultra-masculine fantasy, where consorting with beautiful women is commonplace (never mind that these women are highly likely to have been trafficked and threatened). This worldview is reinforced by constant posts showing that the narco-lifestyle becomes a desirable status to attain, made all the more tantalising by seeing it paraded so openly on social media.

- **Hyper-violence:** For well over 15 years, cartels have engaged in a brutal cycle of one-upmanship online. From the 2000s on, low-resolution videos of rivals being shot, garroted, chainsawed and dismembered were commonly found online. Much as with ISIS and other Islamic extremist organisations, the "inventiveness" showcased in such videos has only increased in Mexico along with image quality. Just as how bodies were left hanging from bridges or dismembered corpses posed in horrific piles in the middle of the street, cartels have used social media to show their innovation in brutality.

- **Shows of strength/Battle footage:** Running gun battles between rival cartels or with security forces are commonplace on social media, even being searchable with a number of dedicated hashtags. Even more common are displays by entire units of a criminal group, showcasing their weapons and body armour. These serve, in part, for a gang to showcase their latest military arsenals.

- **Cults of personality:** Many narcos in leading positions have likely survived for longer than their average compatriots by not showing themselves publicly too often. But this has not prevented some of Mexico's leading criminal figures from having numerous social posts attributed to them through specific hashtags and emojis.

The CJNG's Online Brand

Of all of Mexico's criminal groups, the CJNG may be the best at manipulating propaganda. They do this by focusing on specific categories from the ones listed above, namely hyper-violence, shows of strength/battle footage, and a carefully maintained cult of personality around Mencho *(see chapter on The Cult of Mencho)*.

While there are instances of CJNG members engaging in *narcocultura* promotion or showing off their weapons and cars, other groups have been more active in this, especially within the Sinaloa Cartel.[2]

The CJNG does not have the same origin story and mythos as their Sinaloa rivals. The group was born out of violence and fragmentation. Besides the Cuinis, the CJNG, which Mencho created in 2011, did not come from a single united faction. Ragtag survivors from the Milenio Cartel's wars, synthetic drug cooks working in western Mexico, young men looking for a break in Michoacán and Veracruz, the CJNG was brought together by violence and profit.

This continues to motivate their social media branding, and the CJNG understands that any press is good press.

Sometimes, they don't need to create the buzz themselves. On May 1, 2015, the CJNG carried out perhaps their most well-known act to date: shooting down an army helicopter with a rocket-propelled grenade in Jalisco and killing nine members of security personnel. By inflicting such a deep humiliation on Mexican armed forces, the CJNG hardly needed to post about it on social media. Others did that for them, with headlines proclaiming the threat the CJNG posed to Mexico.[3]

At other times, the CJNG's PR machine quickly swings into action.

In late June 2020, Mexico City's security secretary, Omar García Harfuch, left home to drive to work accompanied by bodyguards around 6 a.m. As his car drove along Paseo de Reforma, Mexico City's main thoroughfare, gunmen hiding in a truck opened fire. Harfuch's car was riddled with bullets, and while he survived, two bodyguards and a passerby were killed.

Harfuch pointed the finger at the CJNG, whom he blamed for making a series of threats against him.[4] The CJNG did not claim or deny responsibility for the attack, but this failed hit marked another escalation in Mexico's war on organised crime. Security analysts viewed this attack as exceptional for the open way Harfuch was targeted on one of the country's busiest roads.

Within weeks, the CJNG doubled down. In July 2020, a video broadcast on social media showed several dozen men armed with AR-15s and grenade launchers and standing outside a fleet of armoured vehicles. The initials of the CJNG were daubed on car doors for all to see.[5]

The message: Come and have a go if you think you're tough enough.

This strategy was repeated a year later.

Amid a brutal turf war around the town of Aguililla in Michoacán with an alliance of rivals known as the United Cartels, the CJNG made another show of force in July 2021. Dozens of vehicles were lined up along a highway near the town and CJNG members were filmed in high-quality video, their faces bare, bristling with weapons.[6]

A CJNG show of force in 2021. Source: Cuartoscuro.

The Name of Mencho

It is currently unknown if the CJNG leader is alive or dead. He has not been seen alive in any form for several years, rumours of his death frequently surface online, and CJNG allies have betrayed the group, claiming that their loyalty was only to Mencho.

His name is often used in CJNG videos to justify or legitimise a wide range of commands or actions by the broader group. These cover a diverse and sometimes bizarre range of topics.

Mencho's mugshot regularly adorns posters hung up in towns across Guanajuato, Jalisco, Michoacán and beyond, where CJNG members gave out televisions, toys, kitchen items and food to local families on various occasions, including Mothers' Day.[7]

Another video from July 2022, showing armed CJNG gunmen, featured a voice coming from off-camera, calling for all of Mexico's cartels to stop harming teachers, doctors and priests. This message came days after two priests were killed in the state of Chihuahua by a local drug lord.

In October 2023, an unsettling video of armed men wearing Halloween masks declared that they would be "purging" almost 30 towns in the State of Mexico, again claiming to be loyal to Mencho.[8]

While these examples were handpicked to showcase the sheer range of incidents to which Mencho's name is attached, they lead to a couple of conclusions.

On the one hand, either Mencho is alive and remains involved in planning or approving CJNG operations at a highly detailed level. On the other hand, different CJNG elements across Mexico have a certain amount of free rein in using Mencho's name and image to further their criminal activities.

Social Media and Video Games for Recruitment

Virtually every social network and instant messaging service available in Mexico, as well as many online video games, has been weaponised by cartels for recruitment.

The statistics are alarming. In 2011, it was estimated that around 35,000 young people had been recruited by organised crime in Mexico.[9] The number has likely soared since. But for a worrying number, their first chance to join cartels like CJNG came online, often in surprisingly straightforward ways.

On Facebook and Instagram, the CJNG has simply placed paid job advertisements. In one such instance, it referred to itself as "the company with 4 letters" and mixed up text and emojis to spell out the initials CJNG. The ads often offered nondescript "security roles", but would provide details about salaries, and perks such as free food and accommodation.[10]

While Facebook and Instagram moved to quickly close accounts linked to such adverts, several cartel-affiliated profiles remained active for months on end without being detected.

Other efforts were more targeted. Young people living on both sides of the Mexico-US border have frequently reported receiving messages on

TikTok, Snapchat, and other platforms, offering them work as *coyotes* (human smugglers) to help migrants across to the US.[11] [12]

Other attempts have been more sinister still.

In October 2021, authorities in the southern state of Oaxaca announced that three children, aged between 11 and 14, had been found after running away from home to join a cartel. They had been found in the city of Monterrey, over 1,300 kilometres away.[13]

While the group that trafficked these specific children has not been made clear, the modus operandi is one frequently used by the CJNG.

In the early hours of the morning, when children are likely to be playing online games unsupervised, they may receive an unsolicited invitation to join a guild or server or private group. The names of such groups may contain the initials of cartels, "CJNG" for Jalisco Cartel New Generation, "CDS" for the Sinaloa Cartel, "CDN" for the Northeast Cartel, etc.

Once inside, criminals posing as teenagers may tell them about the cartel lifestyle, encouraging them to run away from home and promising adventure and wealth. Some of the most played games in the world, including Grand Theft Auto Online or World of Warcraft, have been affected.

And while public pressure has led to these platforms taking action to shut down such content, cartels and their admirers are getting around it with ease.

Simply adding the little purple devil emoji (😈) to the hashtag led to a series of videos where someone was recreating, in painstaking detail, the CJNG's famous displays of weapons and vehicles inside Grand Theft Auto Online.

THE CJNG AND METHAMPHETAMINE

The CJNG has myriad ways of making money. Looking back over the last twenty years of its evolution, methamphetamine may have been the most important for its staying power and profitability. At least, until fentanyl came along.

It did not come to this criminal economy by chance. While the Valencias may have begun with producing marijuana and opium poppy, Mencho's time in Tijuana and California showed him the insane profits to be made from the meth trade, taught him how to make it, and helped him establish the international connections to import the chemicals needed *(see chapter on The Cult of Mencho)*.

The back-and-forth nature of the US' meth epidemic is quite complex. As demand for the drug soared, government agencies sought to control it, and criminal groups innovated to sidestep new regulations.

The demand for other drugs has ebbed. The legalization of marijuana in the US has cut into cartel profits.[1] The rise of cheaply made, highly addictive fentanyl has seen cartels drop the production of heroin, causing devastation for communities of opium poppy farmers.[2]

But far from killing off methamphetamine, the rising market for fentanyl has furthered the demand. And while fentanyl has overtaken meth as a cause of death in large parts of the US, the number of people dying from consuming both types of drugs has soared.[3]

And the CJNG is reaping the profits from both.

A Brief History of Meth

The 1960s and 1970s saw a rise in the use of a range of stimulant drugs known as amphetamines, or *speed*, both legally and illegally produced, in the United States. Athletes took them for performance, truckers to keep driving, and partygoers to keep dancing until the morning light. Alarmed by this spread, the US Food and Drug Administration (FDA) restricted amphetamines to prescription-use only in 1965.[4]

But demand remained, in particular for methamphetamine, which is significantly more potent than most other amphetamines. Continuing to crack down, the US declared key chemicals needed to make methamphetamine as controlled substances, making it difficult to obtain them legally.

Motorcycle gangs in California, especially the Hells Angels, ramped up illegal production. While these gangs had started making illegal meth in the 1970s, production was helped along by an unusual figure.

Production grew to large-scale laboratories, known as mega-labs, that began appearing in the early to mid-1980s. This process was helped along by the likes of Steve Preisler, a chemist from Wisconsin who became known as "Uncle Fester." In 1987, his cookbook *Secrets of Methamphetamine Manufacture* made meth recipes available to all.[5]

Preisler's recipes explained how to extract the main component for meth, ephedrine, from legally purchased items such as cough syrup. This was then to be combined with antifreeze, battery acid or drain cleaner to produce a solid, crystallised form of methamphetamine.

Crystal meth was produced at such a scale that its cooks needed more ephedrine than was available. They turned to their entrepreneurial criminal neighbours to the south. Mexican groups began supplying large quantities of ephedrine in increasing amounts to the Hells Angels and other drug traffickers throughout the 1980s.

Three brothers from the Mexican state of Colima, in particular, took over this trade, moving ephedrine into the US through Tijuana. Their names: José de Jesús, Adán and Luis Ignacio Amezcua Contreras.[6]

These enterprising brothers, who founded the Colima Cartel, were the first to begin creating international supply chains for the chemicals needed to make meth. In the early 1990s, José de Jesús travelled to India, Thailand, Germany, the Czech Republic and the Netherlands to seek ephedrine providers.[7]

But the Colima Cartel was not sending everything north. Keeping a portion of the chemicals for themselves, they began making meth in small facilities in Jalisco, Colima, Nayarit and Michoacán, the very western states that would see the birthplace of the CJNG two decades later.

The Amezcua brothers were early pioneers of the synthetic drug industry that has flooded the US to this day, and which is still concentrated in western Mexico. From their base of operations in Guadalajara, they expanded a network of facilities making meth and continued to send the drug to the United States throughout the 1990s. They were also early partners of the Valencia family in Michoacán, selling their methamphetamine partly to the Milenio Cartel.

Following the arrests of José de Jesús and Luis Ignacio in 1998 and Adán in 2001, the Colima Cartel remained important meth traffickers but saw their influence gradually wane, as more powerful Mexican groups picked up the slack.

Western Mexico, the heartland of the Valencias and the Milenio Cartel, became the country's meth production hotspot. Of 847 meth labs raided by Mexican security forces between 2002 and 2012, close to 90% of them were in Michoacán, Jalisco and Sinaloa.[8]

After the Colima Cartel was dismantled, the Sinaloa Cartel became the dominant producer and exporter of meth to the United States in the 2000s.

The situation further turned to the advantage of Mexican meth producers in 2005, after the United States passed the Combat Methamphetamine Epidemic Act.[9] This further limited the ability of individuals within the United States to buy cold medicines containing ephedrine and pseudoephedrine. Mexico would go on to adopt stricter drug measures of its own in 2007 but, like many of the country's drug laws, this had no discernible effect.[10]

CJNG and Chemical Innovation

The period during which meth became a criminal mainstay in Mexico coincided exactly with Mencho's own rise to power. While his exact activities at the time are unclear, it's highly likely he was refining his knowledge of the meth trade.

He had been pottering about western Mexico, Tijuana and California during the late 1980s and 1990s, learning the ins and outs of the meth trade at the time of the giant California super labs.

He was back in Mexico in the late 1990s, at the peak of the Colima Cartel's production and export to the United States, a time when it also supplied the Valencias.

And he worked for the Sinaloa Cartel when they dominated the meth trade in the mid to late 2000s.

Mencho moved into the meth trade at the right time. In 2011, the global supply chain for crystal meth was focused in Mexico. That year, 56% of all global seizures of methylamine, a chemical commonly used to make crystal meth, were in Mexico.[11]

It was a natural step for Mencho to secure a large portion of this well-established supply chain. Amid the chaos in Jalisco, Michoacán and Colima, the CJNG was able to quickly secure contacts to import chemical precursors from China, lab sites to make the meth in Mexico, and the connections to smuggle it to the US.

The gang was also able to control routes next to and leading from two important ports, Manzanillo and Lázaro Cárdenas, through which chemical precursors entered Mexico. This placed them within a few hours' drive away from most of the labs.

Meth became the first drug that the CJNG could produce and sell in industrial quantities and this largely bankrolled the cartel's expansion in the early years. From 2011 to 2015, dozens of meth labs appeared in the places of origin of the Valencia family and Mencho, such as Aguililla in Michoacán.

Brutal fighting would take place between the CJNG and other groups staking out a claim to the meth trade, such as the Knights Templar.

Smaller facilities in urban areas tended to provide the supply for local consumption while larger kitchens in remote parts of western Mexico would crank out crystal meth in larger quantities to go to the US market. A leaked report from the US consulate in Guadalajara also pointed out that the city's advanced tech sector provided plenty of chemists and engineers who could be lured in to help the cartels make higher-quality meth and safer production lines.[12]

The CJNG would quickly show off its chemical innovation skills. The group took part in an informal competition among Mexican cartels to rapidly raise the quality of crystal meth. The purity of the drug made in Mexico went from 42% in 2007 to 93% in 2012.

By 2015, meth had helped make Mencho and the remaining Valencias immensely rich.[13]

By then, the CJNG's control over the meth trade was so predominant that Mencho invited the remaining Amezcua family members to join the group. The remnants of the Colima Cartel brought with them a wealth of knowledge relating to the production of meth.[14]

A Pillar of the CJNG's Power

The CJNG is commonly described, as other cartels frequently are, as a top-down business-like structure, with Mencho at the top, trusted commanders overseeing crucial parts of its criminal empire, and "employees" making the drugs and selling them.

A look at the CJNG's structures inside the meth trade shows a far different reality. First, the CJNG has always made meth close to "home" in western Mexico. Part of this was a choice based on logistical issues. The ports of Lázaro Cárdenas in Michoacán and Manzanillo in Colima have always been the main entrances for chemical precursors from China, and the city of Guadalajara was a natural point from which to stockpile and distribute drugs.

But beyond this, the CJNG has used the meth industry to maintain connections to the communities that spawned it. Between 2006 and 2018, 439 meth labs were found in Mexico. 254 of them, or 57%, were in Michoacán. Another 159, or 36% of the total, were in Jalisco.[15]

Even the Sinaloa Cartel would place most of its drug labs inside Sinaloa and Sonora, the states it had absolute control of. The heart of Mexico's meth industry never shifted much from its western birthplace, despite a plethora of criminal networks vying for power there and despite other ports closer to the US border.

The CJNG uses a blend of violent intimidation and economic allure to run its meth industry. In southern Jalisco and Michoacán especially, the CJNG allows smaller community-based groups, employed as contractors, to manufacture meth and sell it to the larger cartel.[13]

Local businesses, such as construction and real estate, are then used to launder profits. While the CJNG is known for its diverse financial practices, most of its money laundering schemes are executed close to home *(see chapter on the CJNG's Money Laundering Empire).*

Unlike fentanyl, which, despite a steady increase in addicts in Mexico, remains principally bound for the US, meth is sold in both countries. The CJNG has labs dedicated to either domestic or international production, the University of Toronto found.

But, busting the image of all these labs being hidden far into the mountains, the CJNG has been known to have labs in rural and urban areas with surveillance networks developed specifically to protect each of them. While some are indeed found far out in remote areas, many are hidden inside farms or townhouses.

As a consequence of this focus on western Mexico, communities in the area have also been devastated by meth. According to the country's National Commission Against Addictions, meth was Mexico's second most common substance abuse problem, behind only alcohol. 22.9% of addicts registered in Mexico used meth, far beyond marijuana at 14.3% and cocaine at 9.4%. Fentanyl was not included in the survey.[14]

The Tidal Wave of Meth

The CJNG and the Sinaloa Cartel are responsible for an absolute torrent of methamphetamine crossing the Rio Grande to the United States. From 2009 to 2014, the period in which the CJNG really got going, meth seizures at the Mexico-California border increased by 300%.[15]

The tidal wave of meth hitting the US was just beginning. Annual US seizures of meth at the Mexico border just kept rising, hitting just over 20 tons in 2015, doubling to over 40 tons in 2018, and soaring to a peak of over 90 tons in 2021.

While the exact percentage attributable to the CJNG can only be estimated, they were certainly colossal contributors. In July 2021, 50 tons of benzyl chloride, a chemical commonly used to make meth were seized at the Pacific seaport of Manzanillo, Mexico's largest. In October 2021, the same year as the record meth haul in the United States, the US Treasury Department sanctioned four alleged CJNG members for bringing in precursor chemicals to make meth and fentanyl.[16]

From 2021 to 2023, there was a small drop-off in meth seizures in the US. But this is more than offset by a meteoric rise in fentanyl seizures. Officers at California border crossings alone seized 300% more fentanyl in 2023 than in 2022.[17]

Much like heroin before it, methamphetamine may be starting to feel the impact of fentanyl becoming the dominant opioid in the United States. However, it is a slow burn.

Outside the United States

There were consistent alerts from US and European authorities around 2015 that the CJNG, especially the Cuinis *(see chapter on The Rise of the Cuinis)*, had been selling meth in large quantities to Europe and had travelled there to set up drug labs.[18]

The full details of the CJNG's involvement in the European meth trade are difficult to parse. Mexican traffickers have been found in Europe, especially in the late 2010s, overseeing the cooking of synthetic drugs and training European counterparts on how to produce them in the Netherlands, Belgium and Central Europe.[19]

However, the extent to which Mexico's largest cartels were involved in these deals has not been proved, and other judicial reports have suggested these "cooks" may have been hired in a freelance capacity.[20]

One arrest, in particular, has been connected to the CJNG. In March 2020, Carlos Rubén Ramírez Monroy, a known CJNG operative, was arrested in Romania for trafficking methamphetamine and cocaine into the country. He was later extradited to the US and sentenced to 15 years in prison.[21]

But judicial documents later described him as having coordinated meth deals for the CJNG in the US, Romania and New Zealand. This paints the picture of a trusted figure sent to close deals around the world instead of someone focused on Europe.

The head of port police in Rotterdam said in a 2024 interview that no Mexicans had been arrested in the Netherlands for several years. He speculated that cartel brokers, who once may have flown around the world to supervise drug deals may no longer be necessary as most drug business is now done fully at a distance.[22]

Despite the absence of such arrests, European authorities continue to regularly seize Mexican-made meth, including at the ports of Rotterdam, Valencia, Hamburg and Cork, as well as the airport of Amsterdam-Schiphol.[23]

Connections to Australia have been easier to prove.

Seeing a constant market for meth and ready-made partners in Australian biker gangs, Mexican cartels have been consistent suppliers of the drug down under. Since at least 2016, the CJNG has developed tight working relationships with its Australian counterparts. It began to do so several years after the Sinaloa Cartel had established similar ties.[24]

These ties function similarly to those outlined above, with Mexican groups acting as wholesalers and Australian networks as distributors and vendors.

The complexity and cost of smuggling meth to Australia across the Pacific, often via the US, is more than offset by the scale of the markup synthetic drugs fetch upon arrival. A kilogram of meth can be bought in Mexico for around 650 dollars, but the equivalent amount can fetch up between 185,000 to 230,000 dollars in Australia, according to official estimates.[25] [26]

However, Mexican groups face stiff competition from rivals in Myanmar, who also produce vast quantities of meth for sale in Australia.

And despite these networks having been known about for years, efforts to stop it have failed. Australians consumed a record amount of meth in 2023, according to an analysis of the country's wastewater.[27]

THE CJNG AND FENTANYL

The economics and geopolitics of the fentanyl crisis in the United States were ideal for the CJNG. When demand for fentanyl grew and then exploded from 2016 onwards, the CJNG already had the business ties, the supply chain, the logistics, the production facilities, the corrupt networks and the smuggling partners in place to seize the opportunity.

To the CJNG, when fentanyl demand began to affect heroin, this simply represented a shift to using different chemicals and modified production methods, often at existing facilities. But the basic logistics of its supply chain - ordering fentanyl itself or its chemical precursors from China, putting the finishing touches on the drug in Mexico if needed, and trafficking it into the United States - remained unchanged.

Since its earliest days as the Milenio Cartel, the group had developed the infrastructure needed to back up its interest in synthetics, first with meth, then heroin, then fentanyl.

It had the ports. One of the CJNG's first moves as an independent criminal group in 2012 was to secure its presence at the ports of Lázaro Cárdenas and Manzanillo on the Pacific, and the port of Veracruz on the Gulf of Mexico, diversifying the routes through which it could bring in fentanyl and its precursors.[1]

It also had contacts. In the early 2000s, the Milenio Cartel had close ties to Zhenli Ye Gon, a Chinese-Mexican citizen who pioneered many of the early strategies used to connect Mexican cartels and Chinese chemical companies.[2] And prior to the CJNG's formation in 2011, many of its senior leaders, including Erick Valencia Salazar, alias "El 85," had worked at the port of Manzanillo, ensuring a steady flow of precursors for the Sinaloa Cartel's meth and heroin labs.[3]

This brought them precious ties to China's colossal - and largely unsupervised - chemical industry.[4]

And, especially thanks to the work of the Cuinis (*see chapter on The Rise and Fall of the Cuinis*), the CJNG had extensive networks of corrupt officials and police in Jalisco and Colima through which to begin trafficking fentanyl.

Why Fentanyl?

Fentanyl had hovered on the fringes of Mexico's synthetic opioid industry for a while, making occasional appearances but taking a backseat role to meth and heroin. In 2006, a string of fentanyl overdoses across the northeastern and midwestern US were at least partially linked back to Mexico, according to a situation report by the US Department of Justice. A seizure of 2.6 pounds of fentanyl powder (which reads as almost quaint compared to the monstrous proportions of the current fentanyl epidemic) was made in February 2006 near California's border with Mexico. An investigation led to the dismantling of a fentanyl lab in the city of Toluca, just west of Mexico City, in May 2006.[5]

But experiments with how to mix fentanyl with various drugs had already begun. Overdoses in the US were described in 2006 as having come from "fentanyl powder, fentanyl mixed with heroin, and, to a lesser extent, fentanyl mixed with cocaine."[6]

Over the next decade, fentanyl would feature as a relatively minor participant in US drug statistics. However, opioid analgesics, a category including methadone, tramadol, oxycodone and fentanyl, were already claiming far more lives than heroin. Drug overdoses from opioid analgesics close to doubled between 2001 and 2011, according to the Centers for Disease Control and Prevention.[7]

In Mexico, the CJNG would rapidly awaken to fentanyl's full potential. In 2012, meth was the primary concern for the CJNG and the Sinaloa Cartel alike, as production exploded in Mexico and neighbouring Guatemala. The competitive advantages of meth were becoming clear, and that logic would carry through to fentanyl.

Cocaine is not produced in Mexico, meaning these groups could only act as middlemen and wholesale distributors. The cannabis plant and the opium poppy used to make heroin require land, rain and agricultural expertise while being vulnerable to authorities discovering and seizing plantations.

Synthetic drugs, on the other hand, can be produced indoors in hard-to-detect labs and can be synthesized through a range of methods and chemical precursors.

One important detail needs to be highlighted. In US government reports from the early days of the fentanyl boom, Mexican cartels are described as monolithic corporations, running the entire synthetic opioid fentanyl supply chain: first buying the drug and its chemical precursors from China, pressing it into pills or producing it in Mexico, and then selling it directly to US drug users.[8]

This is not accurate. While CJNG members did make deals to buy fentanyl or its precursors in China and did move it in bulk to the United States, several parts of the process were outsourced. A slew of subcontractors, often experienced drug cooks and chemists, would be provided with the chemical building blocks, cook the desired fentanyl, meth or heroin product in their labs, and then sell it to cartels.

In 2018, a Bulgarian biochemist was even caught running his own fentanyl and carfentanil lab in the town of Mexicali right on the US border.[9]

By 2016, fentanyl was beginning to catch up with heroin, which had "utterly dominated the illegal opioid market for a century," according to a drug policy professor at Carnegie Mellon University.[10]

The Realisation

Overdose deaths involving synthetic opioids, including fentanyl, rose by 73% to 9,850 from 2014 to 2015.[11] Seizures of fentanyl, in various forms, skyrocketed from 934 in 2013 to 13,000 in 2015.[12]

"This category of opioids is dominated by fentanyl-related overdoses, and recent research indicates the fentanyl involved in these deaths is illicitly manufactured, not from medications containing fentanyl," said a White House drug report in 2015.[13]

While heroin was still killing more Americans overall until 2015, the drug in its pure form was gradually being left behind. In March of that year, the DEA would put out a nationwide alert about the dangers of fentanyl, amid a slew of media reports about overdoses spiking in major US cities.[14]

The CJNG's fingerprints and those of their Sinaloa Cartel rivals were all over this. Production labs for meth and fentanyl were largely concentrated in the western states of Mexico, which the two large cartels controlled. The vast majority of seizures at the US border took place in southwestern states, again at border crossings routinely used by the Sinaloa Cartel and the CJNG to smuggle meth, heroin and cocaine.

Various forms of distributing fentanyl were available, making it all the more difficult for authorities to track.

There were two major ways of getting fentanyl to US drug users. The first was to lace it with heroin. According to the DEA's 2016 National Drug Threat Assessment, a kilogram of fentanyl-laced heroin could contain as little as one teaspoon, or 5.69 grams, of fentanyl.[15] In this way, it can enhance the potency of heroin whether it is injected, snorted, or smoked. The resulting mixture is also significantly more lethal.

The DEA and other US institutions now put out regular health alerts warning people to the risks of various fentanyl-based cocktails of drugs, but to seemingly little effect when looking at spiking synthetic opioid overdoses.[16]

But while the DEA noted many users were exposed to fentanyl without knowing it, many addicts were actively seeking the opioid, and choosing traffickers who could provide fentanyl-laced heroin.

The other way to reach the US drug market was to press fentanyl into fake prescription pills, often mislabelled as oxycodone. So rapidly did this modus operandi grow that seizures of thousands of pills, all containing fentanyl, were already being made in late 2015, at a time when the US was still awakening to the scale of the crisis.

Chinese contacts could provide all the equipment and supplies needed for these various methods of distributing fentanyl to thrive. Powdered fentanyl was shipped from China to Mexico along with presses to make the fake pills in the same labs that were producing meth.

But despite even mentioning that some packages of fentanyl crossing the border in 2016 were stamped with the name "El Chapo," the DEA did not list fentanyl among the drugs produced by the Sinaloa Cartel and the CJNG in its 2016 assessment.[17] This was the boom time for heroin. In its 2016 Greatest Drug Threat Survey, the DEA found that 45% of law enforcement respondents listed heroin as the largest threat, followed by meth at 31.8%, and 11% for controlled prescription drugs. Fentanyl wasn't on the list.

By 2017, the secret was out. The Sinaloa Cartel was being challenged openly by the CJNG for control of Mexico's synthetic drug trade. And with fentanyl, the CJNG was looking to steal a march on its larger rival.

"The Jalisco New Generation Cartel are the new kids on the block. One of the issues is that Sinaloa has dominated wholesale and retail [drug sales] in the United States for years. Well, fentanyl would allow the Jalisco Cartel to take over new markets in US territory," Vanda Felbab-Brown, a senior fellow at the Brookings Institution, said in 2017.[18]

Fentanyl first appeared on the DEA's 2017 Greatest Drug Threat Survey, with 6.3% of law enforcement respondents listing it as the largest threat, far behind heroin at 44.1%.[20] Mexican authorities also started becoming more aware of the risk of fentanyl, as seizures soared.

The scale of fentanyl addiction, as well as its lethality, were not fully mapped out that year, as few drug testing facilities had the equipment to check for fentanyl, either on its own or laced in with heroin.

But the DEA was already singling out the CJNG and the Sinaloa Cartel as those likely responsible.[21]

Fentanyl as a New Product

Analogies comparing the actions of criminal gangs to those of legitimate businesses are somewhat overplayed and oversimplified. But here, the comparison holds up.

The CJNG and the Sinaloa Cartel were assigning resources and recruiting more subcontractors to produce more and more fentanyl as pills and laced into heroin. The goal now was to increase the customer base. How? By selling fentanyl masked as heroin and prescription opioids, the drugs with the largest existing number of users.

With fentanyl's potency over 50 times that of heroin, the two could be cut together and split into far more doses, increasing both profits and the potential for addiction. In 2016, DEA spokesman, Russ Baer, told VICE News "that one kilo of fentanyl [at a cost of $3,000-4,000] can produce between 16 and 24 kilos [of drug product], ultimately yielding profits of $1.3 million after it's sold on the streets."[22]

And with fentanyl powder and pill presses coming from China, it was relatively simple to pass off pure fentanyl pills as oxycodone, a highly potent opioid painkiller.

"The drug dealers don't know what they're selling, the consumers don't know what they're buying and putting in their body," Baer said. "Now with the counterfeit opioid labeling, it's an expansion of what is a frankly ingenious marketing technique by these Mexican cartels."

This tapestry of fentanyl cocktails became even murkier as drug traffickers across the United States appeared to make their own concoctions. For example, from 2017 onwards, a string of overdoses was attributed to "gray death," a highly lethal blend of fentanyl analogues, such as carfentanil, heroin, and designer drugs.[23] However, DEA reports indicated that the substances inside gray death varied widely across the country. This means that these were likely local experiments rather than any further innovation by Mexican cartels.

While legal actions against the CJNG were still primarily focused on its role in trafficking meth and heroin, its part in fentanyl trafficking was becoming clearer on both sides of the border. In a 2017 DEA report on Chicago, the CJNG was identified as one of the Mexican drug trafficking organizations most responsible for supplying the city, including fentanyl.[24]

But that year, overdose deaths from synthetic opioids killed more than 28,000 Americans. Fentanyl and its variants were squarely at the heart of this epidemic. In comparison, overdose deaths from heroin peaked in 2017 and have gone down every year since.[25]

In 2018, the role of the CJNG in the fentanyl trade was laid bare as the US poured resources into investigating this threat. The DEA placed the CJNG on par with the Sinaloa Cartel and found alleged CJNG distribution hubs in Los Angeles, New York, Chicago and Atlanta.

By the end of that year, the CJNG was firmly in the US government's crosshairs. In October 2018, Attorney General Jeff Sessions unveiled a raft of sanctions and indictments seeking to "cripple the operations of the CJNG," which was blamed for trafficking tons of "fentanyl-laced heroin" into the US.[27]

Whether these moves had any real impact is debatable. By the time these proclamations were made, several targeted CJNG leaders, including Mencho's son and brother-in-law, had already been arrested. If nothing else, the Sessions-led investigations showed the US had fully recognised the CJNG's role in the country's fentanyl epidemic.

In Mexico, increasing raids on drug labs in Jalisco, Michoacán and other western states revealed a network of dozens of synthetic drug facilities.[28] Although specific groups behind each drug lab are not always easy to identify, seizures were largely based in the CJNG and the Sinaloa Cartel's areas of operation. Reports of seizures show that synthetic labs producing meth and fentanyl for the CJNG were found primarily in Jalisco and Colima, the group's heartland, and the central Bajío region.[29]

This synthetic opioid boom was also taking a grim toll on the local communities in Mexico where these labs were based. Mexican media SinEmbargo reported that certain local residents were strong-armed or tricked into working for the CJNG either as lookouts or as cooks.[3]

There was a fresh challenge in 2019. China banned the production and sale of fentanyl and many variants, known as analogues. While this made it difficult for the CJNG and others to import ready-made fentanyl powder, this modus operandi was already in doubt at the time.

"China's chemical industry suffers from poor regulation, thus allowing fentanyl precursor chemicals…to be diverted into clandestine labs by criminal groups," InSight Crime wrote in 2019.[31]

The Mexican cartels quickly shifted and Chinese vendors, masquerading behind complex corporate entities, continued to provide all the precursors their counterparts needed.

The Boom Years

By 2020, the CJNG was "the greatest criminal drug threat to the United States," according to one DEA statement.[32] In March of that year, a six-month investigation into the CJNG, dubbed Project Python, culminated in a series of arrests and seizures. More than 650 alleged CJNG associates were arrested, and 350 indictments were issued. Large quantities of fentanyl, heroin, meth and cocaine were all seized. The DEA also found that the CJNG had established an important operating centre in Tampa Bay, Florida. Mexico was also on the move, with seizures of fentanyl in Mexico rising by 486% to reach 1.3 tons in 2020 and raids on synthetic drug labs doubling in the country in the same year.[33]

But once again, the scale of fentanyl production and demand likely meant these raids were quickly shrugged off by the CJNG.

In 2020 and 2021, the CJNG continued to expand rapidly across Mexico, taking the fight to the Sinaloa Cartel, especially around Tijuana. Any faint hopes of reversing the fentanyl trend were fully fading.

In fact, the cartel's fentanyl empire was only expanding. While fentanyl was entering the country through several large seaports, the port of Manzanillo in Colima was the jewel in the crown. The port was not safe, as a 23-ton seizure of chemical precursors in August 2019 showed. But far more was coming in than was being caught, as laid bare in US sanctions against CJNG's specific leadership at the port.

But the quest to control fentanyl production sites and trafficking routes had become a cause for violence in and of itself (*see chapter on The CJNG's Many, Many Wars*).

The central state of Zacatecas felt the price of this, as Mexico's fentanyl battlegrounds began to expand from Jalisco and Guanajuato. In 2020, homicides almost doubled to reach 1,244 deaths in one year, by far the greatest increase of any Mexican state that year. Its appealing logistics to the fentanyl trade were at the heart of this, according to the state's security secretary.[35] Five criminal groups, including the CJNG and the Sinaloa Cartel, the Gulf Cartel, the Northeast Cartel and a smaller outfit called the Talibanes, were blamed for the violence.

Zacatecas is an obvious transit point for drugs heading to the United States, located as it is next to heavy drug production spots like Michoacán and Jalisco. Zacatecas has two highways running through it, one connecting the US to Mexico's southern border, the other coming from the port of Manzanillo. The CJNG saw Zacatecas as a natural extension of its fentanyl business, but was never fully able to pacify the state. The fight against the Sinaloa Cartel for control of Zacatecas continued in early 2024.[36]

But no city in Mexico felt the brunt of fentanyl-linked violence more than the city of Tijuana in Baja California. Close to 4,000 people were killed in Tijuana alone in 2020 and 2021, with the CJNG and a smaller allied group, Los Cabos, taking on the Sinaloa Cartel. This patchwork of violence worsened as the Arellano-Felix family, which long controlled Tijuana, broke into two factions, with each supporting one of the larger rivals.

Mexico is Not Immune to Fentanyl

While the large cartels were fighting bitterly for control of Tijuana, the spike in homicides was not entirely due to competition around who could send more fentanyl and meth to the United States.

Earlier in this chapter, we discussed how the CJNG relied on a network of subcontractors to cook and provide it with finished fentanyl or analogues. Smaller, local drug dealers also began buying the excess product from these labs and selling it for themselves.

As smaller and smaller groups began accessing and selling fentanyl, the consequences on Mexico's own population became increasingly dire. Hints of this new horror appeared in Tijuana. Research by the Ramón de la Fuente Muñiz National Institute of Psychiatry in December 2019 found that heroin users in the city were unknowingly being exposed to fentanyl, which was found in most syringes tested in the city.[37] A Vice News investigation in the city in 2021 found a large homeless population growing increasingly addicted to fentanyl-laced heroin or pure fentanyl itself.[38]

Further studies over the years have found a growing number of fentanyl addicts in much of Mexico, first among states along drug trafficking corridors and now spreading more widely. The numbers have remained low, however, and very low compared to the United States.[39]

The traditional narrative is that this was due to leftover drugs as if a percentage of lost merchandise on the way to the US border should be factored in as the cost of doing business. That is in doubt. There is plenty of money to be made by the CJNG and others in selling fentanyl to Mexican addicts. “It's a market designed for this population because it's easier to produce it [because it is synthetic]. You don't have to wait for a [poppy] plant to grow,” one harm reduction coordinator in Tijuana told Vice.[40]

Despite plenty of warnings, Mexico has been shockingly slow in reacting to the dangers of fentanyl production and addiction in its own country. But this is part of an odd culture of denial concerning the scale of the fentanyl problem in Mexico. While admitting fentanyl is trafficked through Mexico, President Andrés Manuel López Obrador has stubbornly refused to accept that it is produced or consumed there.

“We do not produce fentanyl nor have fentanyl consumption. We're really sorry about what is happening in the United States, but why don't they… combat fentanyl distribution?” he said at a press conference in March 2023.[41]

Yet the truth is undeniable. A 2022 investigation by InSight Crime found that ever-higher numbers of bodies presenting as fentanyl overdose casualties were being processed by forensic services in Mexico.[42]

By 2024, López Obrador had begun to change his tune, admitting that while fentanyl consumption remained low, it was “something we have to take great care about.” He also suggested a legal reform banning the consumption of fentanyl in Mexico.[43]

Local sales of fentanyl in Mexico may be a lesser priority for the CJNG, given the profits to be made in the United States. But such denialism from authorities is a gift for these criminal groups, as it prevents a full picture of the fentanyl crisis from being painted.

Besides the obvious humanitarian failure of not helping drug addicts, accurately tracking fentanyl deaths within Mexico could be a powerful tool in tracking changes in where the drug is produced and trafficked.

Same but Worse

The fentanyl crisis continues to worsen, both from a public health and from an organized crime perspective. Over 110,000 Americans died of drug overdoses in the 12 months leading up to September 2023, according to provisional CDC statistics. Synthetic opioids, mostly fentanyl, are connected to around 70% of these deaths.[44]

Attempts by the United States to crack down on Chinese suppliers of fentanyl precursors have continued, but have been met with severe rebuke from Beijing.[45] [46] Seizures of fentanyl at the US-Mexico border reached an all-time high of 12.1 tons in the 2023 fiscal year, up 90% year-on-year.[47]

"Fentanyl is everywhere. It's not just disguised as heroin, but it's also actually present in cocaine and methamphetamine," Dr. Nora Volkow, director of the National Institute on Drug Abuse at the National Institutes of Health, told CNN.[48]

In Mexico, there seems to have been one significant development, however. Some of the country's most prominent cartel groups appear to be turning against fentanyl.

In June 2023, the Scorpions, a powerful faction within the Gulf Cartel, put out a video in which it prohibited the sale or consumption of fentanyl and crystal meth in the northern state of Tamaulipas. The reason: to keep out the CJNG. The Scorpions' video included a message reading, "We don't want the Jalisco here in the state of Tamaulipas, all they do is poison people."[49]

Then in October 2023, banners were put up across Sinaloa. "In Sinaloa, the sale, manufacture, transport or any other business dealing with fentanyl, is strictly prohibited, including the sale of chemicals used to produce it. You have been warned. Respectfully, Los Chapitos," they read. The Chapitos is a collective name used by the sons of former Sinaloa Cartel kingpin, Joaquín Guzmán Loera, alias "El Chapo." They form arguably the most powerful faction within the larger cartel.[50]

While there was immediate doubt as to whether the Chapitos would really give up on the fentanyl trade, given how lucrative it is, the ban was confirmed to be real, at least in Sinaloa. Bodies of alleged transgressors soon began appearing with fentanyl pills dumped on them as a warning. But other reports claimed this was all part of a strategic reset by the Chapitos to shift production elsewhere and keep control of the fentanyl trade.[51] [52]

In order to keep official attention away from their home state of Sinaloa, the Chapitos shifted production to Chihuahua, Puebla, Durango and Nuevo León, according to leading Mexican crime journalist, Luis Chaparro.[53]

He added that high-level military connections had made a deal with the Chapitos for fentanyl production to leave Sinaloa for elsewhere and that, in return, their operations wouldn't be disrupted.

"A top general in Sinaloa made an agreement with Los Chapitos to move all of their production out of state and promised he wouldn't really go after them. Then, he could tell his bosses, 'Well, we couldn't really find any [labs].'

The State of Fentanyl in 2024

As of 2024, there is little cause for optimism.

With American, Chinese and Mexican authorities beginning to pay closer attention to the fentanyl trade, the search for precursor chemicals has gone global.

The judicial cases against several top CJNG brokers have revealed just how broad these relationships were. Over more than a decade, two brothers, Javier and Carlos Algredo Vázquez, set up an extensive trade network for a wide range of chemical precursors. With one based in New York and the other in Mexico, the brothers posed as legitimate chemical importers before being indicted and arrested in 2021.[54] [55]

The full network of brokers and international connections that fuel Mexico's fentanyl trade is only beginning to be uncovered. But a superb investigation by InSight Crime tracked in detail how the Algredo Vázquez went far afield to circumvent growing scrutiny in the US, Mexico and China, sourcing chemicals in India, Turkey, Germany and beyond.[56]

From 2018 to 2021, the Algredo Vázquez brothers moved over 1,400 tons of chemicals to produce methamphetamine, over 1,800 tons to make that methamphetamine more potent and over 44 tons to produce fentanyl.

How their network manipulated weaknesses in the global chemical regulatory system to source specific chemicals from specific countries was mapped out by InSight Crime as part of a lengthy investigation into the global fentanyl supply chain.

Crackdowns, intending to choke the suppliers providing precursor chemicals to the CJNG and others, have continued. In 2023, the US ramped up indictments against a number of Chinese chemical manufacturing companies. But there has been mounting frustration at a perceived lack of action by Chinese authorities to expand its own actions.

And the statistics only show how any efforts to control the fentanyl trade continue to fall short. In the US in 2023, authorities seized over 77 million fentanyl pills and nearly 16 tons of fentanyl powder.[57]

This was not just a yearly record.

It was enough to kill every American man, woman and child.

HOW ELSE DOES THE CJNG MAKE MONEY?

Most commonly associated with drug trafficking, the CJNG's level of territorial control across Mexico has given it the ability to exploit a vast array of varied criminal economies. Extortion and kidnappings can be replicated in any part of Mexico. But many are more localized, providing significant illicit income to the CJNG from targeted opportunities.

Some have received significant attention. The level of violence associated with the CJNG's fuel theft practices in the state of Guanajuato or its systematic oppression of avocado growers in Michoacán have triggered strong state responses. The United States has also moved to sanction networks involved in the CJNG's growing timeshare scam targeting timeshare families.

Others are still not fully understood. There have been sustained allegations that the CJNG sends illicit wildlife products to China in exchange for chemical precursors used to make meth and fentanyl, for example.

In this chapter, World of Crime provides an introduction to the most important ways the CJNG brings in hundreds of millions of dollars besides narcotics.

Avocados

Technically, this falls under the category of extortion mentioned above, but avocados are so closely connected to the origins of the CJNG that they deserve their own mention.

It might break the hearts of the original Valencia family members to see how their criminal descendants in the CJNG abuse and terrorize the avocado-growing communities of Michoacán and neighboring states.

The persecution of avocado farmers, as well as those growing limes, in Michoacán began at scale with a criminal group called the Knights Templar which dominated large parts of the state until the mid-2010s.[1]

Similarly to the extortion business model deployed by the CJNG in Jalisco, the Knights Templar had access to government records, showing the land and number of trees owned per producer. The cartel would then take a cut at each stage of the production process, charging producers a flat fee per hectare, which would be higher if they exported their fruit. When the harvest came, producers would be extorted a flat fee per ton produced. Then, again at the packing stage, each packer was charged per kilo of avocado.

And corrupt authorities both facilitated this process and took their cut at every stage. From 2009 to 2014, the Knights Templar and La Familia Michoacána are estimated to have extorted avocado growers out of at least $154 million a year.[2]

Once the Knights Templar began to lose ground after a bitter war with the CJNG and self-defence groups which began in 2014, there was little relief for avocado growers. By 2019, at least four criminal groups, including the CJNG and former self-defence gangs, were targeting the farmers.[3]

And when they cannot extort, the criminal groups have no problem simply expanding avocado plantations. Legitimate companies or producers can approach them and come to a deal to clear a specific area. While much of the land in Michoacán is protected, such regulations are ignored. Forest cover is burned, anyone living in the area is moved or killed, and new avocado trees are planted.[4] This has only exacerbated environmental damage, and producers complain of crippling deforestation and water problems.

In 2024, the Global Initiative Against Transnational Organized Crime issued a report with recommendations to reduce the instances and impact of criminality on avocado-farming communities.[5]

Despite extensive media coverage and government condemnations, extorting avocado farmers remains a major income booster for the CJNG and is a large reason why it has fought so bitterly to control Michoacán. However, the creation of a new generation of self-defence groups, to whom farmers pay protection, appears to have improved the security somewhat.[6]

Extortion

In February 2024, a CJNG video was published in the central state of Puebla. Its intention was to warn residents of certain cities not to fall for a scam, where a local group, known as La Barredora, was demanding extortion payments from businesses in the name of the CJNG. "We reiterate that we do not demand extortion payments," said the masked and armed CJNG spokesperson.[7]

This was almost comical. Mexico's Financial Intelligence Unit has consistently named the CJNG as one of the foremost culprits in the country when it comes to extortion.[8]

The CJNG has industrialized extortion across its Mexican criminal empire. From early on in its existence, the CJNG saw extortion as a financial pillar which could support its expansion.

It began in Jalisco itself. In 2015, a tequila business owner told Vice that he had been forced to pay 200,000 pesos (around $13,400) a month to the CJNG for two years.[9] This ultimately led him to close his business. While numerous businesses were systematically extorted, the CJNG became skilled at identifying local specialities that could be slowly bled dry.

Tequila producers in Jalisco, avocado growers in Michoacán, fishing communities along the Pacific coast, hotels and restaurants along the Caribbean coast, the CJNG's extortion empire is both expansive and expensive.

Each area of opportunity is evaluated and charged with skill and expertise within the group. In 2022, Mexican newspaper El Economista revealed how the CJNG systematically charges for each head of cattle sent by ranchers in northern Jalisco to the United States. The cartel paid off local officials to access state-run databases tracking the property area and number of cattle owned by each rancher. Market prices were then evaluated to come up with the price the CJNG would charge per cattle.[10]

As per 2022, ranchers had to pay 5 pesos ($0.3) for each of the 100,000 cattle produced in northern Jalisco a year. This accounted for about half of their profits per animal, according to El Economista.

And extortion is adjusted for inflation. Merchants at Mexico City's Central de Abastos, the largest wholesale food market in the world, reported that CJNG-linked extortionists increased their demands by about 5.3% from 2022 to 2023, shortly after taking control of the market's extortion dynamics.[11]

Fuel Theft

For decades, fuel theft, known as *huachicol* in Mexico, was seen as a serious but largely localized problem. Gangs based in communities living near large refineries or along pipelines would control a network of "taps" that they would access at times that fuel was flowing through. This fuel would then be sold on, mostly to nearby residents. While this caused significant losses to Mexico's national oil company, Pemex, there were few reports of associated violence.

Instead, these bands were seen as respected figures, stealing needed fuel for their communities. A religious figure, known as El Santo Niño Huachicol (The Blessed Child of Fuel Theft), would even be created.[12]

In 2001, a band, known as the Chapaductos in northern Veracruz, became the first criminal organization dedicated to oil theft to make national headlines. But these stories focused on how the theft occurred, how the fuel was stored and sold on, and the alleged identities of those involved.[13]

Fuel theft remained a secondary criminal economy in the eyes of the Mexican government until the arrival of President Felipe Calderón to power in 2006. It would become an increasing issue of national importance during Calderón's time in office, as the number of thefts soared and the extent of corruption within Pemex became clearer.

Detected taps of Mexico's pipeline network more than doubled, from 323 yearly in 2006 to around 800 in 2011. The real numbers were likely far higher, as thousands of incidents were reported to Pemex, and numerous petrol stations were shut down or investigated for being supplied with stolen fuel.[14]

The extent of complicit corruption inside Pemex, within which plenty of employees and executives were participating, facilitating, and profiting from theft, also became clearer.

"It started as petty theft by workers and then strengthened into a structure that, from within the oil facilities, involves unionised and trusted employees, contractors, gas station owners, industrialists, pipeline siphoners, transporters, captains and ship crews," according to an investigation by Mexican newspaper Proceso.[15]

Edgardo Buscaglia, an accomplished economist who has studied crime in Mexico, put it even more brutally. "We need to discard the idea that organised crime is organised solely by networks of figures like El Chapo Guzman…the Mexican state operates within Pemex as organised crime. These are criminal networks where all political parties take a cut, economically speaking," he said.[16]

This cash cow would not be stopped. From 2011 to 2016, fuel theft incidents would grow by another 80%.

What provoked this runaway expansion? The larger cartels took notice. Fuel theft was the second-largest moneymaker for criminal groups after drug trafficking, according to senior intelligence officials.[17]

The Zetas were among the first larger criminal groups to strike deals with local fuel thieves. This fit in with their strategy of taking over all established criminal enterprises as they took over new territory in the 2010s.

But the CJNG was on their heels within a few years.

One of the first areas of Mexico to see a rapid rise in violence directly linked to fuel theft was an area in the central state of Puebla known as the Red Triangle. Spread across the eastern part of Puebla, the Red Triangle is home to a sprawling network of gasoline and liquid natural gas pipelines. It is located close to Veracruz, a fortress of the Zetas, which made for easy expansion by the cartel.[18]

Groups with experience stealing fuel were often left to run their operations but had to pay extortionate fees to the Zetas. One *huachicolero* told

Rolling Stone in 2018 he was paying $10,000 a month, likely to a splinter group known as the Zetas Vieja Escuela (Old School Zetas) in Puebla.[19]

The CJNG soon contested the space. In 2018, the group left a number of bodies, often bearing signs of gruesome torture, to be discovered in the Red Triangle. Messages found on the bodies made it clear the CJNG would not allow any oil thieves to operate without their say-so. Violence by the CJNG connected to fuel theft has remained a constant in the Red Triangle since.[20]

But no state has suffered more of the consequences of fuel theft as Guanajuato. In 2018, the state saw the most murders in Mexico with 3,436 homicides, which rose further to 4.964 in 2020.[21]

This period coincided with one of the bloodiest cartel feuds in recent Mexican history as the CJNG sought to claim control of the lavish fuel theft profits to be made from the pipeline network surrounding the Salamanca refinery. The cartel ran afoul of an alliance of local oil thieves, who called themselves the Santa Rosa de Lima Cartel (CSRL), named after the small town where they originated. Their leader, José Antonio Yépez Ortiz, alias "El Marro," seemed utterly unfazed at fighting the larger group.[22]

This brutal campaign made Guanajuato's cities, such as Irapuato, Celaya and León, to be placed among the most violent in the world. Reports of massacres across Guanajuato became increasingly commonplace and extortion became so severe that essential food providers temporarily shut up shop.[23] [24]

Mexico's President Andrés Manuel López Obrador could not just let this pass. Upon taking office in December 2018, he declared that ending oil theft was a national priority. Thousands of troops were deployed to Guanajuato to protect pipelines, the amount of fuel being stolen did drop, and El Marro was arrested in March 2020.[25]

López Obrador cried victory, but this pacification campaign did not last long. The CJNG is the most powerful criminal group in the state and makes lavish profits from controlling fuel theft and drug trafficking routes. But the CSRL has bounced back from the capture of El Marro and continues to control large parts of rural Guanajuato. As of 2023, Guanajuato remained the most violent state in Mexico, with over 21,400 homicides in five years.[26]

However, the quantity of pipeline taps in the state has fallen. In 2023, the epicenter of huachicol had moved to the small state of Hidalgo, which saw almost 3,000 reports of fuel theft. The CJNG is known to operate there in strength, but violence has remained comparatively low, for the time being.[27]

Illegal Fishing

The full scale to which Mexican cartels are directly involved in Mexico's rampant wildlife trafficking has not yet been fully mapped. But one aspect of this ecosystem, the systematic takeover of Mexico's fisheries by organized crime, is becoming clearer.

The encroachment of the Sinaloa Cartel and the CJNG into fishing communities across Mexico, although especially along the country's northern Pacific coastline, has allowed them to profit from the fishing industry, in a number of ways.

Both cartels are increasingly active in extorting fishermen, forcing restaurants and processing plants to buy seafood they provide, and selling in-demand species to China, especially along Mexico's Pacific Coast, according to a 2022 investigation by the Brookings Institution.[28]

Their involvement has both domestic and international impacts. Internationally, Mexican organized crime is cornering the market for numerous species which are wanted by consumers in Asia. The best-known example of this is for the air bladders of the totoaba fish. These bladders are a delicacy in Chinese cuisine, where they are cured and used for soup. Profits can reach tens of thousands of dollars per kilogram. While Chinese buyers used to deal directly with local gangs in fishing communities, the Sinaloa Cartel and the CJNG appeared to have cornered this market.[29]

This business model has since been extended to include sea cucumber, abalone and geoduck clams, as well as more common catch, like lobsters. Mexican Navy seizures of these types of seafood have revealed that these practices are growing along Mexico's coastlines.[30]

In her 2022 report, Vanda Felbab-Brown, senior fellow at the Brookings Institution, reported that cartels were exchanging some seafood with Chinese contacts for chemical precursors to be used to make meth and fentanyl in

Mexico. Although this likely accounts for only a small percentage of the purchase of chemical precursors, it sets a worrying precedent for how Mexican organized crime can sidestep follow-the-money investigations by trading for precursors, instead of buying them outright.[31]

Connections between the drug trafficking trade and the fishing industry run deeper. A 2024 InSight Crime investigation documented how criminal networks use fishing boats to collect precursors from container ships offshore to then bring them ashore in the states of Colima, Sinaloa and Michoacán.[32]

But the cartel control over fisheries stretches far deeper onshore. As explained in the Brookings Institution report, organized crime groups "seek to monopolise legal and illegal fisheries along the entire vertical supply chain."

Fishers are told what to catch and where to fish, are forced to sell either directly to criminal groups or to their appointed representatives, the prices at which fishers sell and businesses buy seafood is set by organized crime groups, and restaurants and food companies may only buy from approved fishers or the cartel representatives. On top of this, organised crime takes a share of fishers' profits through extortion payments. Several fishers who transgressed these rules or resisted have been killed.[33]

Illegal Logging and Timber Trafficking

Controlling and profiting from Mexico's rich forestry resources was a no-brainer for its criminal groups. It was a straightforward way to diversify their criminal portfolio in parts of Mexico they already operated with almost complete impunity.

The Sinaloa Cartel and the Juárez Cartel have set up lucrative operations in the pine forests of Chihuahua, controlling logging operations and sawmills, as well as how the illegally felled timber enters the supply chain.[34]

But the worst of Mexico's illegal logging takes place in states partially or mostly controlled by the CJNG, especially Jalisco and Michoacán, as well as Colima and Nayarit. While private companies have felled trees without permits in these states for decades, criminal groups began taking over control of this criminal economy in 2016.[35]

The modus operandi works as follows, according to a study by the University of Guadalajara. The owner of a forested area is approached and asked to sell their land at far less than market value. Should they refuse, the trees will be felled anyway, without compensation. If complaints are made to federal environmental authorities, those responsible or nearby communities will be silenced through intimidation and kidnapping. Many members of these remote communities in CJNG-controlled areas have fled, and some have been killed.[36]

The CJNG also controls sawmills that cut the felled trees into logs and other forestry products which are then mostly exported overseas through the ports of Manzanillo and Lázaro Cárdenas.

Once felled, the area is not left fallow. Around 100,000 hectares of forestry were cleared in Michoacán between 2000 and 2021, mostly to be replaced by avocado plantations.[37]

This has had a major knock-on effect on local communities, including indigenous populations, who have found their ways of life upended and wildlife. The spread of avocado plantations and the destruction of traditional pine and fir trees have had a significant impact on the iconic monarch butterfly, whose numbers in Mexico have cratered.

Migrant Smuggling

For the CJNG, along with its rivals, profiting from those seeking to reach the United States may have started as a side operation connected to their primary drug trafficking ventures. Facilitating the passage of migrants through Mexico to the United States, these cartels charged hefty sums for what was often promised as safe passage. For the CJNG and rivals who controlled territory along the US border, such as the Gulf Cartel and the Zetas, this 'service' was accompanied by the opportunity to kidnap and extort migrants, or put them to work.

Over the years, the activities surrounding migrant smuggling have progressively taken a darker turn, evolving from mere facilitation to exploitation. Kidnapping, extortion and forced labour became prevalent, with migrants often being the easiest targets. These individuals found themselves caught in a web of organised crime that saw them as commodities.

From 2019 onwards, the "Remain in Mexico" program put in place by US President Donald Trump saw asylum seekers forced to stay in Mexico while their application requests or court cases were processed. This often saw migrants stay in some of Mexico's most violent cities, including Tijuana, Ciudad Juárez or Nuevo Laredo.[38]

But these crimes were not contained to the northern border. The southern state of Chiapas, along Mexico's border with Guatemala, has seen a sharp rise in migrants being targeted for extortion, kidnapping and forced recruitment since 2020, when widespread fighting between the CJNG and the Sinaloa Cartel broke out.[39]

The increase in kidnapping and extortion operations is part of the CJNG's broader strategy to diversify its criminal portfolio and expand its territorial control. Critical to this strategy is the control over key migrant routes, particularly those near the Mexico-Guatemala border in the southern state of Chiapas.

The surge in migrant kidnappings underscores a strategic shift within the CJNG. By abducting migrants, the cartel has found a lucrative income source with relatively low risk, especially compared to the drug trade. Families of the kidnapped, often residing in the United States or the migrants' home countries, are extorted for ransom, under the threat of harm to their loved ones.[40]

Timeshare Fraud

With much of its money laundering activities based in Mexico's tourist hotspots, timeshare fraud has become a sophisticated and lucrative scam for the CJNG, in which it has ensnared numerous unwary individuals. Although the cartel has run these scams for years, it has steadily become one of its main earners. A New York Times investigation in March 2024 found the CJNG was running "dozens of call centres in Mexico that relentlessly target American and Canadian timeshare owners." It was estimated to have netted hundreds of millions of dollars in this way over a decade.[41]

The scheme typically begins with contact from a seemingly reputable firm offering to purchase timeshares already owned by their victims. These fraudsters, linked to the CJNG, create a veneer of legitimacy by using fake contracts, forged official documents and even counterfeit websites mimicking real estate or law firms. Victims are led to believe a buyer is ready to purchase their timeshare for an attractive price, but there's a catch: sellers must first pay upfront fees for taxes, legal services, or other fabricated expenses necessary to complete the sale.

Once these fees are paid, the promised sale evaporates. Attempts to recover funds or further communicate with the scammers are met with silence. The CJNG's intricate network ensures the money quickly disappears.[42]

And it is not just owners of timeshares in Mexico that are targeted, those owning such properties in Jamaica and the United States have also been ensnared.

Complaints related to timeshare fraud have soared by 79% in four years, coinciding with a boom in the overall timeshare industry, with sales reaching $10.5 billion in the US in 2022. Almost 10 million US families own timeshares, giving the CJNG plenty of targets.[43]

The US Treasury Department has repeatedly sanctioned individuals and entities associated with the CJNG and its timeshare scams, but so far, these do not appear to be having any large-scale deterrent effect.

WHERE IS THE CJNG IN MEXICO?

Since the CJNG roared onto Mexico's criminal scene over a decade ago, it has been blamed for soaring violence in every part of the country. Much of this blame is deserved. Like the Zetas before it, the CJNG is in a perpetual expansion mode, picking fights with small local gangs and nationally present cartels alike.

But the truth behind reports of CJNG violence can vary. It is difficult to determine precise patterns or plan security operations based on looking at these incidents. The CJNG produces a high volume of narco-banners and videos across Mexico, all announcing its next moves. These, in turn, lead to a vast quantity of media articles and policy reports, which muddy the waters as to what the CJNG may be planning.

The CJNG, at least externally, seeks to maintain the illusion of a clear-cut chain of command. Many of the videos published by the CJNG are signed with the name of El Mencho and masked gunmen in videos claim to be acting in the name or on orders of the leader.

But given the sheer territory across which the CJNG operates, its localized commanders, or *jefes de plaza,* are likely given broad authority to handle local rivalries and act in the interests of the group.

Drawing conclusions from a single message, or even a handful of messages, is ill-advised. Some isolated announcements can seem to have far-ranging consequences, then quickly fizzle out.

In September 2022, for example, a slew of media reports spoke of the creation of a group, known as *Nueva Alianza* (New Alliance).[1] The name appeared on a narco-banner left in Atizapán, a town just northwest of the Mexican capital. This Nueva Alianza was allegedly formed by members of the CJNG and one of Mexico City's main gangs, La Unión Tepito.[1] This could have been momentous, giving the CJNG a firm base to expand its operations inside the Mexican capital.

But the Nueva Alianza has rarely been mentioned since and may not have lasted long.

In contrast, some more sophisticated campaigns have revealed very real intent.

Major expansions can be accompanied by a more sustained and targeted messaging campaign. Take the CJNG's brutal incursion into Zacatecas in 2020.[2] On April 12, 2020, identical banners were hung up in 17 different municipalities in the state. All bore the same message: "*From today, the state of Zacatecas is represented by the CJNG. We are already here, the kidnappings, extortion and shakedowns are over. We guarantee security and respect to the citizens of Zacatecas.*"

They didn't keep their promise. From November 2020 to November 2021, homicides in Zacatecas rose by 52% as the CJNG expanded rapidly in the state, seeking to control drug routes and secure ideal locations for fentanyl labs.[3]

Since late 2022, CJNG videos and banners have appeared more frequently in Aguascalientes, Morelos, Oaxaca and Puebla. In Morelos, a video saw CJNG troops announce that Mencho now "owned" the state.[4] In Aguascalientes, allegedly corrupt officials were named, shamed and threatened by banners stating "we're coming for you all."[5]

None of these states have been important CJNG battlegrounds in recent years. Such a focus could reveal a potential CJNG aim to expand into new territory.

There is a recent precedent here. The southern state of Chiapas has become one of Mexico's principal criminal battleground states since 2022 after the CJNG moved in to contest migrant smuggling, extortion, and drug trafficking opportunities controlled by the Sinaloa Cartel.[6]

In order to provide some clarity, World of Crime presents an alphabetical breakdown of the CJNG's presence in every Mexican state.

Research for this chapter was completed in March 2024. However, organized crime dynamics in Mexico are highly fluid and the situation in any part of the country can change rapidly. The CJNG's presence in each state is listed as being little, moderate, strong, or dominant.

Aguascalientes: *Strong presence*

With a strategic location in central Mexico and close to the CJNG's heartland in Jalisco and Nayarit, it is surprising that Aguascalientes avoided being a major cartel battleground throughout most of the 2010s.

The Sinaloa Cartel and the CJNG have made tentative forays into Aguascalientes, but without fully committing to the state. In 2017 and 2018, for example, state authorities were on high alert as both cartels announced their expansion in Aguascalientes with banners. Murder rates rose rapidly, but this was attributed to the state being next to Jalisco and Zacatecas. The state's attorney general stated "large cartel structures don't exist" in the state.[7]

This has not proven to be true. In 2020, violence gradually became more pronounced after CJNG banners announced a war against elements from the Sinaloa Cartel and the Talibanes, a Zeta offshoot. But again, no gang gained a dominant presence.

Since 2022, Aguascalientes' status as a battleground state can no longer be denied. Homicides rose by close to 20% and the state finished the year as the 11th most murderous state in the country. The CJNG's sense of ownership was in no doubt. In September 2022, the CJNG posted a video online. It showed the cartel's logo inside a map of Aguascalientes and showed armed men vowing to clean the state of rival gangs and corrupt officials.

A new *narcocorrido* song entitled, *Que empiece el juego* (Let the game begin), all about the CJNG's moves in Aguascalientes was even published on YouTube in February 2024.[8]

Aguascalientes is an important waypoint for drugs heading to the United States. The CJNG, the Sinaloa Cartel, and the Talibanes, a Zeta splinter group, are all fighting to control access to a network of highways that connects the small state to Mexico City and Guadalajara.

Their sustained interest in Aguascalientes may also be connected to fentanyl, which is crossing the state with increasing frequency. Despite state authorities denying that fentanyl is a problem in Aguascalientes, numerous seizures and dozens of overdoses in the last few years paint a different picture.

Most notably, an operator for Los Mezcales, a smaller criminal group from Colima, was arrested in Aguascalientes in September 2022 carrying thousands of fentanyl pills. He allegedly was seeking to expand Los Mezcales' sphere of influence to Aguascalientes, according to the Defence Ministry.

Baja California: *Strong presence*

The state of Baja California, especially the city of Tijuana, is one of the main smuggling points for drugs entering the US. Since the late 2010s, it has been a focal point for the CJNG-Sinaloa Cartel war taking place across Mexico, which has made Tijuana one of the deadliest cities in the world. Tijuana saw around 1,800 murders in 2023, down from over 2,200 in 2022.

Mencho has a longstanding relationship with the state, as he repeatedly crossed the border there in the 1980s and 1990s when he was selling marijuana and meth in San Francisco. To break the Sinaloa Cartel's dominance there, the CJNG struck a deal with remnants of the Arellano-Felix family, once-powerful drug lords who ran the Tijuana Cartel. In 2016, narcobanners declared the birth of the Tijuana Cartel New Generation (CTNG).

In spite of this declaration, the CJNG has struggled to maintain permanent alliances in Baja California. The CTNG does not appear to have been active for a long time, as scant mention has been made of this alliance since. The Cabos, a smaller gang in Baja California, were also allied with Mencho until a brutal separation in 2019.

In 2024, both the Sinaloa Cartel and the CJNG continue to fight viciously for control of Baja California's border crossings, especially through the port of San Ysidro, which connects Tijuana and San Diego and sees millions of fentanyl pills smuggled into the US every year.

Similar to other perpetual battlegrounds in Mexico, it is likely that Tijuana simply has too many criminal elements involved for any single actor to take over for long.

Baja California Sur: *Moderate presence*

Historically, Baja California Sur (BCS), best known for its tourist hotspot of Los Cabos, has had low violence rates. Located across the Gulf of California from the state of Sinaloa, it has been dominated by El Chapo's Sinaloa Cartel for much of the last two decades. The group's monopoly over drug trafficking in BCS helped the violence stay down. But analysts stated the Sinaloa Cartel relied on a horizontal partnership with local groups, rather than strong top-down leadership in BCS.

In 2016, perhaps motivated by El Chapo's extradition arrest, the CJNG moved in. BCS became a battleground state for the Sinaloa Cartel-CJNG war, with homicides soaring from 177 in 2015 to 788 in 2017.

But in the years since, this petered out rapidly. Just 23 homicides were registered in BCS in 2023, with several months seeing no murders at all. With BCS among the most peaceful states in the country, it seems the CJNG maintains a small presence there, especially in Los Cabos, but does not see the state as a strategic priority.

Campeche: *Moderate presence*

The CJNG has been linked to isolated instances of violence in the state of Campeche, according to police records. The state's location on the Gulf of Mexico and next to Guatemala could make it a desirable location for drug trafficking, migrant smuggling and contraband. But for the most part, it has avoided the worst of Mexico's violence.

Four people were killed in a shootout in Campeche in January 2023, but while media reports blamed this on the CJNG and the Chapitos, no evidence of this has been provided. The CJNG has also been connected to illegal cigarettes partially produced in Campeche.

In contrast, Campeche's neighbouring state, Chiapas, saw a severe escalation in violence in 2022 and 2023 as the Sinaloa Cartel and the CJNG battled tooth and nail for control of criminal economies along the Guatemala border. Campeche could suffer from an overspill of this ongoing violence.

Interestingly, Campeche also has an almost unique criminal economy in Mexico: piracy. The state and its neighbour Tabasco are hubs for the offshore oil and gas industry, with hundreds of oil platforms off its coast. Hundreds of attacks on oil platforms and ships have been registered, with well-informed and armed thieves stealing fuel, pumps, breathing equipment, and other items.

Chiapas: *Strong presence*

Over 780,000 people entered Mexico as unauthorized migrants in 2023. Those crossing the Guatemalan border into the southern state of Chiapas risked stumbling into one of Mexico's latest hubs of violence.

Since 2022, parts of Chiapas have become a battleground as the CJNG and the Sinaloa Cartel clash to control several lucrative criminal economies. These include drugs smuggled over land from Central America or arriving by sea onto the coast of Chiapas. The record flow of migrants through Chiapas also provides cartels like the CJNG with opportunities for extortion, kidnapping and forced recruitment.

The CJNG developed its presence in Chiapas and Guatemala simultaneously, as it emerged in 2021 that the group had been quietly expanding its network of drug trafficking contacts in the Central American country for several years.[10]

Since 2022, violence with the Sinaloa Cartel has displaced thousands in Chiapas, especially around the border town of Frontera Comalapa. Thousands of residents have been temporarily displaced and the CJNG has been largely blamed by locals for ramping up the violence, according to crime reporter Ioan Grillo. A group of civilians recruited into the CJNG has allegedly been helping the cartel take over local criminal economies and calling themselves Maiz, short for Mano Izquierda (Left Hand).[11]

Not all of these recent recruits may be aiding the cartel willingly, as residents fleeing the violence have also reported that the CJNG had increased the forced recruitment of locals to fuel their battles against the Sinaloa Cartel.

The war in Chiapas may indicate a worrying long-term trend in Mexico: the factors that have driven violence at its northern border for decades are being replicated on its southern frontier.

Chihuahua: *Strong presence*

As one of Mexico's most strategic drug trafficking hubs, boasting highly coveted border crossings with the US like Ciudad Juarez, Chihuahua is consistently one of the country's most violent states.

The CJNG has maintained a constant presence in Chihuahua, but its power in the state has largely relied on an alliance with La Linea, a powerful local force that controls much of the drug flow entering the US between Ciudad Juarez and El Paso. La Linea and the CJNG first united around 2017 and appear to have battled groups connected to the Sinaloa Cartel ever since. Further south, CJNG operations have been reported inconsistently in cities such as the state capital, Chihuahua, and Parral.

Coahuila: *Moderate presence*

Coahuila is a highly desirable slice of criminal real estate, with hundreds of kilometres of a desert border with Texas. However, the CJNG has only had limited success in entering a state far away from its power bases. Coahuila also counts on a heavy presence by the Sinaloa Cartel, the Northeast Cartel and well-armed police squads, which have been frequently accused of moonlighting as drug traffickers.

The CJNG has made announcements about its presence in Coahuila but does not appear to have succeeded in creating a foothold in the state.

Colima: *Dominant presence*

Outside of Jalisco and Michoacán, Colima is the state where the CJNG and its Milenio ancestors have the longest history. The port of Manzanillo is Mexico's largest and has been used for decades as an entry point for fentanyl and chemical precursors used to make methamphetamine and fentanyl.

The CJNG's control of the port is regularly challenged, making Colima a hotbed of violence.[12] In 2016, the CJNG defended itself against incursions by the Sinaloa Cartel and the Zetas. And while the Zetas have faded, the Sinaloa Cartel continues to challenge Manzanillo. In 2022, the Mezcales, a smaller Colima-based gang, turned on the CJNG, claiming Mencho was dead. This led to a brief outbreak of violence until the Mezcales leader was arrested.

Durango: *Moderate presence*

Durango is one of the only states in the country where the CJNG has not been reported to have much of a presence.

The northern reaches of Durango are part of the Golden Triangle, one of Mexico's principal production areas for marijuana and opium poppy. Durango is one of the Sinaloa Cartel's main bastions and would be a tough nut for the CJNG to crack. But with the two groups fighting each other in Zacatecas just to the south, an extension of that violence to Durango is not out of the question.

Guanajuato: *Dominant presence*

Since 2018, the industrial state of Guanajuato has seen more murders than any other Mexican state. Its cities such as Irapuato, Celaya, and León are listed as among the most dangerous in the world. But why?

The CJNG targeted Guanajuato early in its expansion across Mexico. Containing the vast Salamanca refinery, Guanajuato is a center for fuel theft from pipelines, known as *huachicoleo*, which is a major criminal economy. Furthermore, Guanajuato has courted international automotive investments. Its business landscape has made it an ideal location for criminal gangs to ramp up local drug sales and extortion.

In 2018, the CJNG made a renewed push to control oil theft in the state and ran up against an alliance of local gangs specialized in fuel theft, known as the Santa Rosa de Lima Cartel. For a brief time, this became the most violent criminal feud in the country.

Since the capture of the Santa Rosa de Lima's leader, known as El Marro, in 2020, the alliance has dwindled but remains a threat.

In 2022, the Sinaloa Cartel made a push into the south of the state, opening up yet another front against its old rival. Guanajuato also has the grim record of being the most dangerous state in Mexico for police, with over 300 officers killed between 2019 and 2023.

Guerrero: *Strong presence*

The state of Guerrero provides perhaps Mexico's most complicated criminal panorama. According to the Crisis Group, a patchwork of over 40 criminal groups, large and small, fight for control of marijuana and opium poppy production, heroin trafficking, extortion, illegal mining, illegal logging and cocaine and chemical precursors entering through the Pacific Coast near Acapulco.[13]

Larger gangs have fragmented into smaller outfits, fighting brutally for a slice of this criminal buffet. Community self-defence groups have popped up, but many have entered criminal activities.

The CJNG has played its part in all this. In 2019, it entered northern Guerrero and rapidly faced off against a collection of rivals in a conflict that spilled over from neighbouring Michoacán. Since 2022, a flip-flopping relationship between the CJNG and La Familia Michoacna has seen the gangs fight, then make peace, and potentially fight again.[14]

In 2023 and early 2024, the main conflict appeared to be between La Familia Michoacana, and local groups, Los Tlacos and Los Ardillos. The complexity of Guerrero's criminal dynamics and entrenched local groups make it unlikely the CJNG will be able to dominate the state.

Hidalgo: *Strong presence*

Hidalgo is usually one of Mexico's quieter criminal states. It is home to extensive theft from gasoline and liquid petroleum gas pipelines connected to the refinery complex at Tula but its homicide rate has remained comparatively low.

In December 2022, a CJNG faction known as Grupo Pantera released a video announcing their arrival to Hidalgo on orders of Mencho.[15] Since then, government officials in the state have acknowledged that CJNG is present, especially in towns with oil pipelines. While violence has not flared up in Hidalgo so far, there is potential for conflict between the CJNG and local gangs such as Los Hades, especially as the state has become the epicentre of fuel theft in the country.

Jalisco: *Dominant presence*

The CJNG has a curious relationship with Jalisco. It became the group's "home state" out of convenience as that was where a power vacuum presented itself after the death of Sinaloa Cartel chieftain, Ignacio Coronel, in 2010. Mencho initially agreed to run the state under the supervision of the Sinaloa Cartel, although that pact did not hold for long.

The CJNG controls the interior rural parts of the state, including areas near the border with Colima where Mencho is believed to commonly reside. But in the capital, Guadalajara, and around the fringes of the state, it faces several conflicts.

In Guadalajara, it faces low-level but regular interference from Nueva Plaza, one of the first examples of fragmentation within the CJNG. A group of aggrieved lieutenants struck out on their own in 2017 and allegedly received support from the Sinaloa Cartel, although Nueva Plaza has never been a real threat to the CJNG. The Sinaloa Cartel has made incursions into northern Jalisco, and the Cárteles Unidos have operated in several communities in southern Jalisco, seemingly to block CJNG access routes into Michoacán.

Puerto Vallarta, one of Mexico's most popular tourist destinations, is also an important base for the CJNG where it launders money through hotels and other businesses and engages in timeshare fraud.[16]

Mexico City: *Strong presence*

Analyzing organized crime in Mexico City is always a curiosity. The CJNG, as well as the Sinaloa Cartel, is regularly connected to criminal events in the capital but in a limited fashion. In 2020, the group was linked to a series of attacks against La Unión Tepito, one of the strongest home-grown Mexico City gangs. But the CJNG was allegedly arming rivals of La Unión Tepito rather than intervening directly.

Yet, the CJNG has carried out spectacular attacks of its own in the city. In 2020, the cartel tried to assassinate Mexico City's public security secretary, Omar García Harfuch, firing hundreds of bullets at his car as it passed along one of the capital's main thoroughfares. Harfuch was hit three times but survived. Two police officers and a passer-by were killed.[17]

In late 2023 and early 2024, the CJNG was connected to violent incidents in the neighbourhoods of Iztapalapa and Tlalpan. An extortionist group, allegedly connected to the CJNG, was also reported to have taken over the shaking down of merchants in Central de Abastos in the capital, the largest wholesale market in the world.

These incidents are likely to remain the norm. While most of Mexico's major cartels have a presence in the capital, the sheer size, the number of criminal opportunities and the participation of localized gangs make it a tricky position for the CJNG to take over Mexico City.

Michoacán: *Strong presence*

The CJNG has thrown money, munitions and men at the perpetual battleground state of Michoacán for years, yet has never come close to taming it.

There is a strong sense of ownership for many old hands among the CJNG to reclaim Michoacán. In the avocado-growing communities around Aguililla and Uruapan, the Valencia family formed the Milenio Cartel, which would grow to become the CJNG. Mencho himself was born near Aguililla and the CJNG has fought hard to reclaim it.

Beyond territorial loyalty, Michoacán presents a unique criminal opportunity: the systematic and ruinous extortion of avocado growers, whose produce fetches a kingly price in the US.[18]

But it has run into dogged opposition from a long roster of opponents. Driven out of Michoacán by the Zetas in the mid-2000s, the Valencias have tried to take it back regularly. The original thorn in their side was La Familia Michoacana (LFM), a group of allies turned rivals. After LFM weakened in 2011, a faction known as the Knights Templar arose. Their war with the CJNG dominated Michoacán until around 2016. Since 2017, the CJNG has faced strong opposition from Cárteles Unidos (CU), an alliance made up of local gangs, Los Viagras and Cartel del Abuelo, remnants of the Knights Templar and self-defense groups.

The Mexican army has sought to pacify the deadliest areas of Michoacán, including Aguililla occasionally, but troops regularly come under attack.

Michoacán has been Mexico's most untamable frontier for decades. Since the birth of the Milenio Cartel, a rotating roster of criminal groups from the Zetas to the Familia Michoacana to the CJNG have fought to control it. There is little indication any winner will emerge in the near future.

Morelos: *Strong presence*

The small southern state of Morelos is in the unenviable position of being on a large drug trafficking route between Mexico City and Guerrero, a historic cultivation spot for opium poppy and an entry point for cocaine and chemical precursors for the production of meth along the Pacific coast. As the demand for heroin has collapsed with the rise of fentanyl, groups have changed tactics, moving increasingly into extortion. La Familia Michoacana has been present in much of Morelos, but the CJNG declared in 2023 that they would be paying more attention to the state to allegedly stop extortion.[19]

Morelos closed 2023 with a historically high number of murders.

Nayarit: *Strong presence*

A popular tourist destination nestled on the Pacific coast and sandwiched between the states of Sinaloa and Jalisco, Nayarit has been a playground for Mexico's two largest cartels, although neither has been able to completely control it. The state is infamous for having a series of highly corrupt politicians, including some with very close financial ties to the CJNG.

In 2017, the CJNG fought a brutal campaign against remnants of the Beltrán-Leyva Organization in Nayarit. Their goal to expand into the state was allegedly supported by then-governor Roberto Sandoval and his attorney general, Edgar Veytia. Both Sandoval and Veytia were later arrested and charged in part for a range of criminal connections to the CJNG, including bribery, drug trafficking and money laundering.[20][21]

However, the CJNG's push into the state was not entirely successful. The group mostly projects its power in the south of Nayarit, which is close to the CJNG's base in Puerto Vallarta, Jalisco. The CJNG has been connected to timeshare fraud, a scam where owners of timeshare apartments are contacted by false buyers, convinced to accept an offer, and then pay some fees to close the deal, after which the buyers disappear.

Nuevo León: *Strong presence*

Containing Mexico's second-largest city of Monterrey and close to the US border, Nuevo León is one of the wealthiest states in the country. Its criminal fate has most often been tied to the neighbouring state of Tamaulipas, a major drug trafficking hub controlled by the Gulf Cartel and the Northeast Cartel. The latter in particular has expanded strongly into Nuevo León in the last decade, ramping up killings of rivals and police officers.

While the CJNG is not a dominant player in Nuevo León, it has ramped up incursions into the state. In 2024, narco-banners declaring the arrival of the CJNG were spotted in towns west of Monterrey.[23]

Its push into this criminally crowded state has allegedly been supported by an alliance with the Metros, a breakaway faction of the Gulf Cartel.[24]

Nonetheless, drug trafficking dynamics in Nuevo León remain highly fluid and can change rapidly amid shifting alliances and enmities.

Oaxaca: *Moderate presence*

The CJNG has had a persistent but quiet presence in Oaxaca for years, at least compared to its activities in certain other states. Since at least 2017, CJNG narco-banners have appeared in parts of the state, vowing to clean up extortionists, thieves and kidnappers. In January 2023, a video message was published by CJNG gunmen, vowing to take large parts of Oaxaca, including the Isthmus of Tehuantepec.[25]

The Isthmus, referring to the narrowest point in Mexico between the Gulf of Mexico on one side and the Pacific on the other, is valuable criminal real estate. It is an ideal corridor for drug trafficking as well as migrant smuggling, with the Oaxacan coast a popular destination for smugglers to leave those seeking to make their way to the US.

Oaxaca is a complex state for the CJNG to navigate, with a high number of local gangs who defend small turfs, a diverse network of indigenous groups, and the presence of rivals like the Sinaloa Cartel. As of early 2024, both groups are involved in a violent feud in neighbouring Chiapas, and there is a risk the fighting could spill over into Oaxaca.

Puebla: *Strong presence*

Puebla presents many attractive qualities for an enterprising cartel. It has an extensive pipeline network filled with oil and natural gas, making it one of the most prominent states in Mexico for fuel theft. Violence connected to the CJNG in Puebla's Red Triangle, an area containing a large network of oil and gas pipelines in the east of the state, has been ongoing since 2017.[26]

It is along a major drug trafficking corridor, as evidenced by seizures of fentanyl, methamphetamine, cocaine and heroin. Indeed, Puebla has also seen a handful of fentanyl laboratories found within its borders.

The CJNG has taken advantage of all of these, making Puebla key to a number of its criminal economies, but ultimately the organisation faces significant local challengers. In October 2023, a video appearing to be by the CJNG declared a clean-up around the town of San Martín Texmelucan. However, authorities soon said they had arrested those responsible and claimed the video was filmed by a gang only pretending to be from the larger cartel.[27]

There have been several real instances of copycat groups pretending to be the CJNG, as smaller gangs seek to profit or cow rivals based on the fearsome reputation of the larger cartel.

Querétaro: *Moderate presence*

Criminal economies in Querétaro appear quite similar to those of its neighbour, Guanajuato. Although Querétaro has no refinery, it has a pipeline network ripe for being tapped by fuel thieves. Located in the centre of Mexico, it is a logical waypoint for drugs going north. Yet, for several decades, it has enjoyed the reputation of being one of Mexico's safest states, with levels of violence far below the national average.

An urban legend in Mexico has it that the country's largest criminal groups, including the Sinaloa Cartel, the Gulf Cartel, and the Zetas, jointly agreed that Querétaro would be a no man's land, a haven where cartel bosses could send their families to live quietly in peace.[28]

There is little evidence behind this story, but Querétaro has indeed remained unusually peaceful as Mexico's homicides soared. In October 2023, a CJNG video announced the alleged arrival of the cartel in the state. And violence did reach record levels in Querétaro in 2023, which some observers attributed to clashes between the CJNG and the Santa Rosa de Lima Cartel, spilling over from Guanajuato.

Quintana Roo: *Strong presence*

The CJNG is just one of several major criminal groups seeking to expand across Quintana Roo, Mexico's Caribbean jewel which contains the tourist meccas of Cancun, Playa del Carmen, Cozumel, and Tulum. Due to the cash-friendly nature of the tourist industry, Quintana Roo had long been a money laundering hotspot but violent organized crime has been increasing rapidly there in the last decade.

In 2019, the CJNG assassinated El Buda, an experienced operative who allegedly controlled the Sinaloa Cartel's drug trafficking interests along Mexico's Caribbean coasts. He was killed in Quintana Roo's capital of Chetumal, a port city which has been used to bring cocaine, weapons and migrants into Mexico.[29]

Further north, the CJNG has made plentiful profits from the tourism industry. It has developed an extensive extortion network, shaking down hotels, resorts and other businesses connected to the massive tourism industry. It fights brutally to distribute drugs to visitors from abroad, with several killings in popular resort towns linked to local drug sales. And finally, the CJNG has brought its timeshare scam to Cancún and owns telemarketing companies that defraud plenty of victims, especially in the US and Canada.[30]

San Luis Potosí: *Strong presence*

Sandwiched next to Guanajuato and Zacatecas, San Luis Potosí is a tempting target for the CJNG. Yet, it has not been able to fully control this sprawling central state which is criss-crossed by important drug trafficking routes. Additionally, thousands of migrants cross San Luis Potosí every year heading for the US border, becoming potential targets for extortion and kidnapping.

From at least 2015, the CJNG has been reported as seeking to wrest control of San Luis Potosí from groups already present there, especially the Gulf Cartel. It has not, to date, been able to do so.

Besides the Gulf Cartel, the CJNG has faced resistance from a slew of smaller groups forming in San Luis Potosí and neighbouring states. Grupo Sombra, an offshoot from the fragmenting Gulf Cartel, appears to maintain strong control of areas along San Luis Potosí's border with Veracruz. Two other Zeta cast-offs, the Talibanes and the Alemanes, have also clashed with the CJNG in the state.

Sinaloa: *Little presence*

Despite its early days as an underling and ally to the Sinaloa Cartel, the CJNG has not set up a foothold in its rival's home state. The Sinaloa Cartel has two major factions, one led by the Chapitos, the sons of Joaquín Guzmán Loera, alias "El Chapo," and the other by El Chapo's old business partner, Ismael Zambada García, alias "El Mayo."

Both control significant territory and resources within Sinaloa and enjoy significant local support among the population.

While there have been sporadic reports of CJNG activity in southern Sinaloa, these do not appear to have significantly disrupted the Sinaloa Cartel's stronghold on its turf.

Sonora: *Little presence*

This northern state, covering a large portion of the Mexico-US frontier, is one of the most regular crossing points for drugs, including fentanyl, and migrants into the US. However, it is firmly in the grasp of two of CJNG's enemies.

Located between Sinaloa and Baja California, Sonora has been a stomping ground for the Sinaloa Cartel and the smaller Caborca Cartel, connected to infamous Mexican kingpin, Rafael Caro Quintero. Sonora remains one of the most violent states in Mexico.

Reports by InSight Crime blame this on internal divisions in the Sinaloa Cartel, attempts by the Chapitos to take over Caborca Cartel territory along drug trafficking routes and a huge surge in human smuggling.[31]

The CJNG activity has been sporadically reported around the San Luis Rio Colorado border crossing into Arizona, but a major presence of the group at this important hub for drug trafficking into the US remains unlikely.

State of Mexico: *Strong presence*

The CJNG has lengthy connections with the State of Mexico, also known as Edomex, which almost surrounds the capital. Back in the days of the Milenio Cartel, the state was a main exit route for marijuana, heroin, meth and cocaine being moved out of Michoacán and Guerrero. It was then one of the battleground states in the CJNG's brutal war with the Knights Templar until 2017.

Since 2017, the State of Mexico has remained one of the country's most complex criminal states, with plenty of opportunities for drug trafficking and extortion. It is also a necessary staging point for many criminal groups wishing to operate in Mexico City. Additionally, the state has seen numerous corruption scandals, tying ruling officials and police to criminal groups.

The CJNG has had a constant presence here but has struggled to stand out. Over the years, it has battled La Familia Michoacana in the west of the state and Zeta offshoots to the east. An alliance with one of Mexico City's main gangs, La Unión Tepito, was briefly reported in 2022 but may not have lasted.[32]

In 2023, La Familia Michoacana appeared to be making significant advances in becoming the dominant criminal group in the state, but this may not last.[33]

The State of Mexico may be connected to virtually every criminal economy in the country. It wraps its way around three-quarters of Mexico City, it is a hub for drug trafficking and production, contraband and human smuggling, and it has a lengthy history of politicians all too willing to work with organised crime.

Tabasco: *Strong presence*

Located on the southern side of the Gulf of Mexico, Tabasco is a small state and a gateway to Mexico's offshore oil infrastructure. While Tabasco has escaped the worst of Mexico's cartel wars, violence remains persistently high. It is an epicentre for the kidnapping of migrants who enter Mexico through Tabasco's remote border with Guatemala.

Its oil industry makes it a natural focal point for fuel theft, and the state is a base for piracy attacks on offshore oil facilities. There are also regular seizures of cocaine, meth and marijuana.

The CJNG is heavily involved in all of these criminal economies and fights to remove local opposition. While it has battled Zetas' splinter groups in Tabasco in the past, the CJNG has been embroiled in a feud with a different gang, known as La Barredora. In February 2024, a CJNG video announced one of its familiar "clean-ups" in Tabasco.[34]

Tamaulipas: *Strong presence*

For close to a century, the US-Mexico border in the state of Tamaulipas was guarded by the Gulf Cartel or its smuggling forebears. This automatically made the group one of Mexico's criminal elite, as it controlled access to the US at the all-important Nuevo Laredo, Reynosa and Matamoros border crossings. In the late 1990s, the Gulf Cartel created the Zetas, a squad of hitmen made up of former Mexican commandos. This led to a brief boom period for the Gulf Cartel, followed by a slow process of fragmentation propelled by a war with the Zetas and the arrest of several top leaders.

The state of Tamaulipas would be a warren of Gulf Cartel factions vying for control during this time. The CJNG spotted an opportunity and moved in. While the CJNG has had a presence in the state for years, it ramped up its activities there in 2023. An alleged alliance with the Metros, a Gulf Cartel faction based in Reynosa, has allowed the CJNG to push into the north of the state. US authorities in Texas have reported seeing a rapid rise in seizures of fentanyl coming from Tamaulipas, another telltale sign the CJNG may be expanding there.[35]

However, despite being fragmented, the Gulf Cartel factions remain deeply entrenched, as does the rival Northeast Cartel. Removing this opposition and dominating Tamaulipas will be a tough task for the CJNG.

Tlaxcala: *Little presence*

In 2022, a map presented in a US congressional report claimed that Tlaxcala was one of only four Mexican states in which the CJNG was absent.

Since then, however, the CJNG has begun to show interest in Tlaxcala, just east of Mexico City.[36]

CJNG narco-banners have been put up, threatening businesses and senior government officials for allegedly working with organized crime. Feuds between the CJNG and fuel thieves in neighbouring Puebla also have the potential to spill over into Tlaxcala, which has seen an increase in pipeline taps in recent years.

Veracruz: *Strong presence*

After the CJNG were firmly established on the Pacific Coast in 2012, they made a beeline across the country to the eastern coast. Their goal: the state of Veracruz, with a coastline stretching almost 600 kilometres along the Gulf of Mexico, and the port of the same name. Controlling that asset would give the CJNG a crucial route to the sea on both oceans, allowing it a far larger range of options for trafficking drugs to the US and for smuggling in chemical precursors. Veracruz was also a bitter battleground state in the cartel's campaign against the Zetas, who had begun fragmenting in 2012.

In the years since, the CJNG has remained one of the strongest criminal actors in Veracruz, especially in the south of the state, which connects to other hubs for the cartel.

However, the north of the state remains one of the CJNG's most persistent battlegrounds. It has not been able to clear out the dogged presence of smaller groups which have fragmented off from the Zetas and the Gulf Cartel. More recently, a new alliance calling itself the Cartel Mafia Veracruzana appears to have gathered several smaller outfits to compete against larger cartels.[37]

Yucatán: *Moderate presence*

Yucatán has remained Mexico's most peaceful state for years. Located on the northern edge of the Yucatán Peninsula, the state is not connected to the country's main trafficking or smuggling routes. There have been occasional reports of CJNG and Sinaloa Cartel activity, but neither group appears to heavily invest in their presence there. However, the state of Yucatán has seen a continuous increase in money laundering schemes discovered there, either through shell companies or through its popular tourist industry.

Zacatecas: *Strong presence*

Since the CJNG became fully formed in 2012, homicides in Zacatecas have tripled. And while violence has gone down slightly since a peak in 2021, the state remains fiercely contested by the CJNG and the Sinaloa Cartel, as well as smaller local gangs.

It is a transport nexus with highways heading to the US border, making it crucial for drug trafficking routes.

In 2019, the Sinaloa Cartel reinforced its operations in Zacatecas to control drug flow to the north and to set up fentanyl labs in the centre and south. In 2020, the CJNG moved in to contest these criminal economies, announcing its arrival with a highly coordinated campaign of narco-banners.[38]

Killings of criminals, rivals and police officers have soared, making Zacatecas one of the focal points of Mexico's war between the Sinaloa Cartel and the CJNG.

Since then, Zacatecas has remained a major hub for fentanyl production, making it all the more valuable to both sides.[39]

THE CJNG ACROSS THE AMERICAS

The international actions of Mexican cartels, especially in the US, are the subject of much speculation. Statements from US authorities and lawmakers often describe the CJNG as being directly, almost intimately, responsible for the deaths of tens of thousands of Americans.

But neither the CJNG nor any Mexican criminal group is controlling individual drug sales at street or city level. They sell drugs wholesale to locally based networks who know their customer base, as well as where to sell narcotics, and how to price them.

Comparisons drawing parallels between criminal networks and corporations have become a cliché, but please indulge one more.

The cartels are not gas stations, providing a service on a street corner. They're Big Oil, manufacturing the products.

The CJNG's actions worldwide reflect this analogy. Whether buying cocaine in South America or selling fentanyl in the US, it acts as a wholesaler. It buys in bulk and sells in bulk. It may have trusted partners and distributors across the world, but will not hesitate to change new ones if it's good for business.

Unfortunately, this is not often reflected in public statements. A recent indictment against CJNG-linked drug traffickers showed how such statements can lead to misconceptions.[1]

On April 1, 2024, the US Department of Justice (DOJ) announced that 41 people had been charged for trafficking cocaine, fentanyl, heroin and meth in the Texas cities of Houston and Galveston and distributing them across the US. They all "allegedly operated under the overall control of the CJNG," read the press release.

They were described as "Jalisco Cartel associates" by Attorney General Merrick B. Garland and as part of the "Jalisco Cartel's trafficking network," said Deputy Attorney General Lisa Monaco.

The alleged leader of this gang, Roque Zamudio-Mendoza, who remains at large in Mexico, is described as "the main source of drugs smuggled into the United States."

"The Jalisco New Generation Cartel casts a dark shadow that extends far beyond the borders of a single nation and into the streets and communities like Houston and beyond," said Alamdar S. Hamdani, US Attorney for the Southern District in Texas, at a parallel press conference about the same operation.[2]

These descriptions raise more questions than they answered.

By what metric was Zamudio-Mendoza the largest drug smuggler to the United States? Over what timeframe? For which drugs?

Were all 41 people arrested active CJNG members, or were some American drug dealers who bought Mexican drugs? Did they buy exclusively from the CJNG or did they buy from whatever wholesaler could provide drugs at the lowest price? How exactly are they inside streets and communities?

While such flowery public statements are usually backed up by indictments and court records that provide more specifics, these are not easy to find.

Outside the US, the CJNG presence becomes even trickier to prove. Rumours of Mexican "control" in other parts of Latin America are usually exaggerated, with the arrest of a broker or the seizure of a Mexico-bound shipment blown out of proportion.[3]

The exception is Guatemala, a long-time retreat for generations of Mexican criminal groups, where the CJNG has made physical inroads and struck alliances with Guatemalan counterparts to take over drug trafficking routes in the country.[4]

This chapter does not look at the CJNG's presence in Africa, Asia, Europe and Oceania. While CJNG brokers making drug deals, laundering money or buying chemical precursors have been seen or arrested around the world, these factors are explored elsewhere in this book.

Here, we break down how the CJNG operates closer to home in the US, Canada and selected countries in the Americas.

United States

Taken out of context, a DEA map tracking the presence of Mexican cartels in the US seems ripped out of a sci-fi movie, in which major American cities have been invaded by powerful enemy armies.

The CJNG absolutely has a presence across the US, with gang members taking care of drug distribution or money laundering. However some context is needed to distinguish between real cartel activity and hearsay.

Drug Distribution

The CJNG has hubs across the US, often in major cities, where it stockpiles drugs coming over the border and coordinates sales to partners in neighbouring states. In 2020, authorities involved in Project Python, a vast coordinated action against the CJNG in the US, reported that the cartel had hubs in Los Angeles, New York, Chicago, Houston and Atlanta.[5]

These cities all offer significant logistical potential, due to the presence of thriving local drug trafficking networks and ease of access to other parts of the country. The CJNG has had lucrative partnerships with large gangs in highly populated areas, including with Dominican groups in New York and the Norteños gang in California.[6]

However, these American gangs are rarely tied to one supplier and may buy drugs from competing Mexican groups at different times, especially in larger cities with a large customer base.

However, other US cities, including far smaller ones, have also been reported as either CJNG hubs or as being fought over by Mexican cartels, including Roanoke, Virginia; Fayetteville, North Carolina; and Gulfport, Mississippi.[7]

The exact involvement of the CJNG in these cases becomes much harder to verify. For example, media reports in late 2023 pointed to the CJNG running a violent meth ring in Port Orchard, a city of around 17,000 people, connected to Seattle by ferry.[8]

"A Mexican super cartel brought its deadly drugs and violence to the tranquil and remote waterfront community of Port Orchard, a 90-minute ferry ride west of Seattle," read an article in the Louisville Courier-Journal which is part of a long-running investigation into the CJNG.[9]

"The cartel, known as CJNG, set up a meth conversion lab here years ago as part of a Western Washington drug cell that pummelled the region with millions of dollars worth of heroin, meth, cocaine and fentanyl-laced pills," it continued.

Court documents paint a different picture. Instead of the CJNG actively taking control of drug production in this remote part of America, it appears a local trafficker bought meth made in Mexico concealed in candles then extracted the meth and cooked into crystal form in Port Orchard.

This is not to diminish the horrific role Mexican cartels play in fuelling the US drug epidemic. The town of Port Orchard has seen several overdose deaths linked to fentanyl and meth, including an 11-year-old girl in 2021.[10]

However, understanding the exact role that the CJNG and other Mexican groups play in the American drug crisis is crucial.

Money Laundering

The enormous profits generated from drug sales need to be laundered, and CJNG uses various schemes to do so within the U.S. This includes funnelling money through front businesses, real estate, or trade-based money laundering schemes. *(see chapter on the CJNG's Money Laundering Empire).*[11]

Much of these efforts centre around getting the profits generated by drug sales back to Mexico without being detected. Sophisticated trade-based money laundering networks have been set up to turn US dollars into Mexican pesos, through seemingly legitimate cross-border commercial transactions. These usually rely on skilled middlemen who manipulate these trades, as well as private American companies, who may not even be aware of their involvement in anything illegal.[12]

Arms Trafficking

A map based on DEA information on the CJNG's arms trafficking networks. Source: CBS.

Hundreds of thousands of firearms cross from the US into Mexico, providing the overwhelming majority of weapons used by the CJNG and other cartels.

The most popular way of doing this is through "straw purchases," where American citizens with no criminal record legally purchase firearms and sell them to cartel members who bring them back to Mexico. While many such purchases happen in towns along the US-Mexico border, some are coordinated from further afield.

In December 2021, a Mexican citizen living in Portland, Oregon, was found guilty of acquiring hundreds of semi-automatic rifles and other firearms for the CJNG through both "high-volume straw purchasers and recruiters of new straw purchasers."[13]

Another way involves the use of "ghost guns," a term referring to firearms built by buying the unfinished frame, also known as a lower receiver, and then machine-tooling other gun parts necessary to complete it. These frames could be more easily bought and traded as they did not meet the definition of a firearm.[14]

As early as 2014, Mexican authorities found CJNG members assembling AR-15 rifles made from incomplete frames and using a tooling machine to finish them off.[15]

In 2022, the administration of US President Joe Biden introduced legislation designed to block both of these avenues, raising penalties for straw buyers and seeking to close the ghost gun loopholes.[16]

Canada

Of Mexico's two largest cartels, the Sinaloa Cartel seems to have entered the Canadian market first. El Chapo's group is known to have a direct relationship with the Rizzuto crime family based in Montreal as well as the Canadian branches of the Hells Angels biker gang.[17]

The death of mafia boss Vito Rizzutto in 2013 appears to have left a void in the Canadian drug trafficking world, especially in the east of the country. In partnership with a new coalition of Canadian criminals known as the Wolfpack, the Sinaloa Cartel continued to dominate the cocaine supply to Canada, according to an excellent book on the Canadian drug trade by journalists Peter Edwards and Luis Nájera.[18]

Much of the drugs sent to Canada were sent from Chicago, a city with a strong Sinaloa Cartel presence and plenty of options for getting narcotics over the border.

But the CJNG was not far behind. As Edwards and Nájera note, Abigael González Valencia, Mencho's right-hand man, entered Canada on a false passport in 2014 likely in search of new business.

A decade on, the CJNG appears to do brisk business with Italian mafia groups in Canada. In January 2024, American, Canadian and Mexican police carried out a joint operation called "Dead Hand."[19]

It revealed how a drug trafficking network, involving Canadian trucking companies, was moving cocaine, meth and fentanyl from the CJNG in Mexico to several major Canadian cities, including Montreal, Toronto and Calgary.[20]

Buyers included the Rizzuto crime family and the Hells Angels, the same customers that bought from the Sinaloa Cartel over a decade earlier.

Colombia

The epicentre of the global cocaine market has shifted in a major way to Europe and away from the US. However, Mexican cartels remain significant buyers of cocaine, as evidenced by their involvement in Ecuador *(see below)*.

Between 2018 and 2022, at least 40 suspected brokers from Mexican cartels were detected in Colombia negotiating drug deals with a number of Colombian criminal groups.[21] These include the Clan del Golfo (Gulf Clan, not to be confused with the Mexican group of the same name), the Ejército de Liberación Nacional (National Liberation Army - ELN) and splinter groups from the now-demobilized Fuerzas Armadas Revolucionarias de Colombia (Revolutionary Armed Forces of Colombia - FARC).

In a shift away from the 1980s and 1990s when the Colombian drug trade was largely controlled by the Medellín and Cali Cartels, Mexican cartels have a greater choice of potential partners in a more horizontal market. This is especially true since cocaine production has been reaching record highs in the 2020s.

And Mexican groups are not just passive buyers. Brokers from the Sinaloa Cartel and CJNG have reportedly been pushing for innovations, contributing to the development of new strains of coca leaf with a higher yield. In turn, this leads to a higher quantity of cocaine being produced at a higher degree of purity, according to a Reuters investigation.[22]

The CJNG's forebears in the Milenio Cartel had direct links to Pablo Escobar and the Medellín Cartel decades ago. But it didn't stop there.

Former Milenio Cartel boss Óscar Nava Valencia revealed to a US court that Abigael González Valencia, the head of the Cuinis *(see chapter on The Rise and Fall of the Cuinis)* had forged ties with a Colombian drug trafficking clan known as the Rastrojos long before the CJNG even existed.[23]

Nava Valencia stated that he had personally invested in three shipments of Colombian cocaine, weighing 1.5 tons each, which Abigael had been in charge of bringing to Mexico between 2006 and 2007.

As the Rastrojos lost power after a series of arrests in 2012, the CJNG and Sinaloa Cartel appear to have then done regular business with different groups, including the Ejército Popular de Liberación (Popular Liberation Army - EPL) and the Gulf Clan, Colombia's largest drug trafficking group.[24] Given the latter group's continued control of prime coca-growing areas and drug trafficking routes in Colombia, the Gulf Clan is likely a regular cocaine seller to the CJNG and Mexico.

Ecuador

Ecuador does not produce cocaine. Ecuador does not consume much cocaine. Yet outside Colombia and the United States, cocaine passes through Ecuador than any other country in the world. It is, to use a phrase coined by InSight Crime, a "cocaine superhighway."[25]

While the flow of cocaine through Ecuador has been happening for decades, its criminal underworld has been transformed in the last four years. Prior to this, a small number of Ecuadorean kingpins and criminal gangs dealt with the Colombian FARC to move cocaine relatively quickly and peaceably from the Colombia-Ecuador border to Guayaquil, a major port city where the drugs could be shipped to Mexico, the United States, or Europe.

Names such as Wilder Emilio Sánchez Farfán, alias "Gato Farfán," once Ecuador's most prolific cocaine trafficker, and the Choneros, the country's first modern drug gang, made their fortunes off this ability.[26]

This changed in 2021. The Choneros and a number of their sub-gangs fell into a brutal civil war that would leave hundreds dead behind bars and thousands dead on the streets of Ecuador. Suddenly, the number of Ecuadorean gangs that foreign traffickers could deal with exploded.[27]

The Sinaloa Cartel appeared to continue an existing working relationship with the Choneros. Both the CJNG and Sinaloa Cartel also worked with Gato Farfán. In February 2022, the US government sanctioned Gato Farfán for working with both Mexican cartels, including sending "representatives of his organization to Mexico to meet with members of the CJNG…to import multi-ton quantities of cocaine into Mexico from Ecuador."[28]

The CJNG made a deal to buy cocaine from the new kids on the block, a gang known as the Lobos. Along with a number of other loyal gangs, the Lobos actually founded a faction named after their Mexican contacts: Nueva Generación (New Generation).[29]

Banners appearing with this name or videos tagged with it led to a false narrative. While the CJNG has made cocaine deals with the Lobos and its allies, and while it has provided the Lobos with weapons and ammunition, the CJNG does not control Nueva Generación in Ecuador.

"The Mexican cartels may buy cocaine from one gang in one part of Ecuador, and from a different gang in another part of the country. They will work with anybody as long as the cocaine keeps flowing," said one Ecuadorean security analyst, who asked to remain anonymous.

However, this still makes the CJNG a bitter threat to Ecuadorian democracy. The quantity of cocaine passing through Ecuador has seen brokers from many foreign actors, including Mexican, Italian, Albanian and Montenegrin drug traffickers, set up in the country to do business.[30]

Despite having a limited physical presence in Ecuador, these actors have driven much of the security breakdown in the country by providing local gangs with the cash and weapons they need to threaten the rule of law.

Guatemala

Since at least 2019, the CJNG has made steadily more ambitious incursions into Guatemala, using it as a staging area to take control of cocaine shipments reaching Guatemala, by sea, land, and air along both the Atlantic and Pacific coasts.

In 2019, Guatemalan prosecutors listened in on phone conversations between a Guatemalan drug ring and a suspected member of the CJNG. While the CJNG member was based in Mexico, prosecutors revealed that it was believed he had been appointed to oversee cocaine shipments arriving on Guatemala's Pacific coast.[31]

This theory gained credence in 2021 when Guatemalan investigators identified another Mexican national and confirmed CJNG member collaborating with a domestic gang of drug runners in the province of Petén and a key cocaine trafficking spot on the Mexican border.

But the CJNG would soon move beyond relying on these envoys to Guatemala. According to the US State Department, the CJNG has also set up shop in Guatemala's northwestern province of Huehuetenango and established a close drug-trafficking alliance with the Huistas.[32]

The Huistas were a good choice as partners. Veterans of Guatemala's cocaine trafficking networks, the Huistas have used their presence in Huehuetenango to their full advantage. Far removed from Guatemala's seats of power, this province has long been a transit destination for people, contraband and drugs. The Huistas are well-connected to political and business elites in the area and have proved to be strong logistical partners for the CJNG, coordinating cocaine shipments from Guatemala to Mexico.

The Huistas are not necessarily the most exclusive partners, however. Knowing their value as the main criminal gang in Huehuetenango, the Huistas have moved significant amounts of cocaine across the border for the Sinaloa Cartel as well.

There remain some doubts about how extensive the CJNG's presence is in Mexico. "There is no permanent cell [of Mexican cartels], but links with Guatemalan drug trafficking clans," said Dr. José Andrés Reyes Valenzuela, a criminologist at Guatemala's Da Vinci University.[33]

That theory would be tested in July 2022 when CJNG gunmen reportedly opened fire on a convoy belonging to Guatemala's President Alejandro Giammattei. The president was not present at the time, but his personal guards spotted an armed convoy while travelling through the village of La Laguna close to the Mexican border. The gunmen in the convoy ignored orders to stop and opened fire. Nobody was killed, but one Mexican citizen and alleged CJNG lieutenant was arrested, while the rest of the convoy fled over the border to Mexico, according to the Guatemalan military.[34]

It is unlikely the CJNG were planning to murder Giammattei directly, although their motivations are not clear for the attack. However, such a brazen show of force fits perfectly into their usual headline-grabbing tactics in Mexico.

Cocaine is not the only reason for the CJNG's presence in Guatemala. In 2023, violence flared up in rural border areas of Mexico's southern state of Chiapas as the Sinaloa Cartel and the CJNG fought for control of ever-popular smuggling hotspots. A network of border towns around the village of Frontera Comalapa has been held by the Sinaloa Cartel to bring drugs, weapons, and migrants across the border. But in June and September 2023, police reports indicated the CJNG was succeeding in pushing its rivals out of this area to take over criminal economies coming from Guatemala for themselves.[35]

ESSENTIAL RESOURCES

The bibliography for this guide runs into hundreds of entries. To keep this book of manageable size, the complete and detailed bibliography can be found on World of Crime's website at

https://worldofcrime.net/cjngsources.

Below, we include some crucial resources in English and Spanish that are of paramount importance to understanding the CJNG and its trajectory.

Uppsala Conflict Data Program - Jalisco Cartel New Generation

https://ucdp.uu.se/actor/1151

How Mexico's Cartel Jalisco Nueva Generación Rules, Vanda Felbab-Brown, The Brookings Institution, 2022

https://www.brookings.edu/articles/how-mexicos-cartel-jalisco-nueva-generacion-rules/

The Brutal Rise of El Mencho, Josh Eels, Rolling Stone, 2017

https://www.rollingstone.com/culture/culture-features/the-brutal-rise-of-el-mencho-196980/

La metanfetamina y el CJNG. Análisis de una reconfiguración del mercado de sustancias ilegales en el occidente mexicano, Nancy Estrella Chávez Llamas et al, Centro de Investigación y Docencia Económicas, 2021

https://revistas.uaa.mx/index.php/caleidoscopio/article/view/3362

The Flow of Precursor Chemicals for Synthetic Drug Production in Mexico, InSight Crime, May 2023

https://insightcrime.org/wp-content/uploads/2023/05/The-Flow-of-Precursor-Chemicals-for-Synthetic-Drug-Production-in-Mexico-InSight-Crime-March-2023-3.pdf

Violent and Vibrant: Mexico's Avocado Boom and Organized Crime, Romain Le Cour Grandmaison & Paul Frissard Martinez, Global Initiative Against Transnational Organized Crime, 2022

https://globalinitiative.net/wp-content/uploads/2024/01/Romain-Le-Cour-Grandmaison-Paul-Frissard-Martinez-Violent-and-vibrant-Mexicos-avocado-boom-and-organized-crime.-GI-TOC-January-2024.pdf

Mexican Cartels: An Encyclopedia of Mexico's Crime and Drug Wars, David F. Marley, ABC-CLIO, 2019

https://www.amazon.com/Mexican-Cartels-Encyclopedia-Mexicos-Crime/dp/1440864756

Los Malditos: Crónica negra desde Puente Grande, J. Jesús Lemus, Penguin Random House, 2019

https://www.amazon.com.mx/Los-malditos-2a-Edici%C3%B3n-Cr%C3%B3nica/dp/6073143389

El amo de Jalisco: Un gobierno con estructura criminal, Ricardo Ravelo, Editorial Inefable, 2023

https://www.amazon.com.mx/El-amo-Jalisco-gobierno-estructura-ebook/dp/B0CP7694L8

Printed in Dunstable, United Kingdom

78991714R00097